dependent local politics in gland and Wales

e book deals with the distinctively local
ects of British local politics — councillors
hout a party affiliation, and ratepayer
vements. The factors which affect the
comes of electoral contests between
ependents are explored and the distinctive
terns of decision-making which often develop
councils controlled by independents are
alysed. With reference to two case studies, it is
ued that both the outcome of elections and
e decision-making process are more
predictable on nonpartisan councils. The
sons for the variations in the success of
epayer movements are examined: two case
dies of successful movements are presented.
e political implications of the 'ratepayers'
volt' of 1974 are also discussed. The book
ncludes with an evaluation of attempts to
plain the persistence of 'localism' in British
cal politics.

Related Saxon House Monographs

The British MP 1945-75
C. Mellors

The British People: their voice in Europe
The Hansard Society

People and Parliament
J. Mackintosh

The British Right
N. Nugent and R. King

Trade unions and pressure group politics
T. May

INDEPENDENT LOCAL POLITICS IN ENGLAND AND WALES

To Maggie

Independent local politics in England and Wales

WYN GRANT

SAXON HOUSE

Published by
SAXON HOUSE, Teakfield Limited,
Westmead, Farnborough, Hants., England

ISBN 0 566 00183 7

Manufactured in England by Short Run Publishing Services
Printed and bound by Ilfadrove Limited, Barry, Glamorgan, S. Wales.

Contents

Preface

This monograph has its origins in a doctoral thesis undertaken at the University of Exeter under the supervision of Mr Jeffrey Stanyer. I have continued to benefit from Mr Stanyer's guidance and advice. Chapters Two and Three of the book are substantially based on my doctoral thesis, but the rest of the material is new. I am grateful to the University of Warwick for giving me two terms' sabbatical leave to undertake the task of researching and writing this monograph and to the Warden and Fellows of Nuffield College, Oxford, for granting me study facilities during the Michaelmas Term, 1976. The Nuffield Foundation provided me with financial assistance which enabled me to carry out the study of two independent councils reported in Chapter One; I am grateful to the members of two councils 'somewhere in England' for their cooperation. I am especially grateful to Ian Robinson of Brunel University for carrying out the secondary analysis of the Eastleigh survey reported in Chapter Four. Professor Hugh Berrington and Professor George Jones made a number of helpful comments on earlier versions of the manuscript. Any errors that remain are, of course, my own responsibility.

Wyn Grant
Leamington Spa,
April 1977.

Introduction

This monograph is about the continuing resistance to the ' "nationalisation" of local politics' [1] in Britain. It attempts to explore one aspect of the differences between local political behaviour and national political behaviour. It does so by exploring two related phenomena: the persistence of independent or nonpartisan [2] control of a large number of local authorities; and the resilience of 'purely local parties', particularly various kinds of ratepayer movement. Independent councillors and 'purely local parties' are generally united by their shared distaste for party politics in local government. They are both manifestations of 'localist' values, defined by Young as 'the emotive symbolisation of the values of the small place'. [3] It must be emphasised that localist values are not confined to independent councillors and 'purely local parties'; as Young notes, 'the orientation is shared by those who profess all party labels and none'. [4] Nevertheless, it is the opponents of party politics in local government who have most to gain from the survival of localist values and who therefore are the most spirited defenders of such values.

As Young points out, diversity and community are the first victims of party intervention. [5] Without a sense of community and a genuine diversity between communities, it is impossible to maintain a coherent defence of localism. In this analysis, nonpartisanship — the belief in the desirability of the absence of party politics from local government — is taken as the core value of localism. The ultimate test of the uniqueness of the locality is its ability to generate its own form of politics without reference to national party divisions. This is not to deny that other values may be relevant to an understanding of 'localism'; clearly an image of diversity in terms of 'the elite actor's conception of the spatial boundedness of his community' [6] and a belief in the legitimacy of the 'government of the locality with respect to other extra-local or supra-local governments' [7] are important. It is rather harder to accept Young's argument that anti-professionalism is a component of 'localism'; it is often present, but it may be counterbalanced by the effects of 'ministerialism' on independent councils (see Chapter One) and 'community conservationism' among ratepayer movements (see Chapter Three).

In selecting nonpartisanship as the core value of 'localism', it is not argued that the local branches of the national political parties do not defend local interests or that they automatically adhere to a nationally derived perspective on local problems. However, as the Layfield Report points out, 'There are powerful pressures in society for more uniformity of provision, stimulated and expressed by well-organised and informed bodies of professional and other interests.' [8] Independent and ratepayer councillors represent a countervailing force. The continued existence of independent and ratepayer councillors signifies that local political systems are capable of generating a distinctive political life of their own. The disappearance of such councillors from local politics would not mean that localist values also disappeared,

1

but it would be a significant step towards the nationalisation of English and Welsh local politics.

Local government reorganisation had the effect of significantly reducing the number of local authorities controlled by independents. Immediately before reorganisation, independent councillors had an overall majority on thirteen English counties and were the largest single category on five others; in Wales, they had an overall majority on eight county councils and were the largest single category on one other. [9] In the first elections for the reorganised counties held in 1973, independents won control of only two English counties (Cornwall and the Isle of Wight) and three Welsh counties (Dyfed, Gwynedd, Powys; they were also the largest single category on one English county (Salop) and one Welsh county (Clwyd). However, on fourteen of the English and Welsh counties elected in 1973, independents remained a significant force in so far as they held the balance between Conservative and Labour, although in some cases they shared this pivotal position with the Liberals. In the majority of cases, independent councillors placed in this position chose to support the Conservatives. For example, 'In Cheshire the elections left the Conservatives short of a majority by two seats. They took control with the help of the five Independents, two of whom had not been opposed by the Tories in the elections.' [10] One independent councillor who had defeated a Conservative became a committee vice-chairman. However, independent councillors were not always as well disposed to the Conservatives. In Humberside, 'During the county election campaign, there was considerable hostility between the Conservative Party and the Independent candidates, and this was transmitted to the council chamber, to the extent that Independent councillors have often supported the Labour Party, with the result that despite its slender overall majority the Labour Group has only been defeated once in a vote in the chamber.' [11]

The 1977 county council elections in England and Wales saw a further significant reduction in the number of independent councillors. However, although independents made 17 gains and 143 losses, with many of the losses resulting from 'changes of label' from independent to Conservative, independents remained the third largest category on the county councils, holding 390 seats in the shire counties and five in the metropolitan counties. Although independents lost control of the Isle of Wight and lost their largest group status in Clwyd, they still controlled four county councils (Cornwall, Dyfed, Powys, Gwynedd), only one less than Labour.

Although independents no longer dominate county councils in the rural shires in the way that they used to, independent councillors retain a significant proportion of seats at the district council level. In 1976, after the district council elections of that year, forty-seven district councils in England and Wales had an overall majority of independent councillors (12.7 per cent of all district councils); independents were the largest single category on another fourteen councils. Thus, independents had a substantial influence on sixty district councils in England and Wales (16.5 per cent of all district councils; 22 per cent of all non-metropolitan district councils).

2

The data base for this study is largely confined to England and Wales, although much of the analysis could be applied to Scotland. One factor which makes it difficult to assess likely developments in Scottish local politics is the uncertain future relationship of Scotland to the rest of the United Kingdom. If devolution (or independence) led to the re-creation of smaller local authorities in Scotland, independent councillors might enjoy something of a revival. As it is, independents are more important at the district council level in Scotland than in England and Wales; after the 1974 elections, they controlled twenty-one of the fifty-three district councils (39.6 per cent) and were the largest single category on one other district council. [12] The 1977 district elections in Scotland did not fundamentally change the pattern of independent predominance in the rural areas. Independents also controlled in 1977 the three most rural regional councils (Highland, Border and Dumfries & Galloway) and the three all-purpose island authorities.

It may be objected that these independents are simply Conservatives who prefer to retain an independent label in areas where there is no serious challenge from an opposition party or where electors are more inclined to vote for an independent candidate than one with a party label. Undoubtedly, many independents are Conservatives in national politics, although they certainly cannot all be so easily classified. Stanyer points out that 'In the case of north and west Devon and central and north Cornwall many of the Independents are Liberals rather than Conservatives, whilst in parts of Wales, where the Conservative Party is very weak, independents are likely to be Labour, Liberal or Nationalist in national political orientation.' [13] Certainly, there is evidence that some independents are in fact Labour supporters in national politics. [14]

A number of studies have shown that independent councillors are often drawn from a different social background from Conservatives and have different attitudes towards key local issues. A study of Ashford found that Independent councillors drawn from the local business community had significantly different views from the professional and managerial Conservatives who replaced them on the key issue of town expansion. [15] Jennings has recorded how the shift of power from Independents to Conservatives in one rural county involved 'the replacement of a landed gentry by younger, more middle class "town Tories" '. [16] On the first Humberside County Council, the Independents were of similar social origins to the Conservatives 'but their rural backgrounds in most cases bring with them political attitudes different from those of the urban middle classes, despite common national political beliefs. On issues such as the replacement of rural schools or the provision of meals on wheels, the Labour Party has had the support of some Independent councillors in defeating Conservatives opposition to their policies'. [17]

Even if the majority of independent councillors are Conservatives in their national political affiliation, the fact that they call themselves independents has significance for the kinds of decisions they take and the way in which they take them. This point is explored more fully in Chapter One when it is argued that councils made up of independents have a more unpredictable decision-making process than councils controlled by a party group.

Independent councillors are largely concentrated in rural areas; ratepayer and other 'purely local party' councillors are found in both urban and rural areas. There are fewer ratepayer etc. councillors than independents; in 1976 there were some 384 'purely local party' councillors on district councils in England and Wales and 36 in the London boroughs. Ratepayers won 28 seats in the 1977 county council elections, a slight increase on the 19 they held previously. However, their significance cannot simply be measured in terms of the limited number of seats they hold; a political group which holds only a small number of seats on a local authority can hold the balance of power between the major parties. For example, when Ratepayers held the balance of power between Conservative and Labour on the London Borough of Havering, crucial support for a comprehensive education scheme 'came from a few Ratepayer councillors elected from working class wards who refused to vote with their colleagues from other wards'. [18] Perhaps even more important, the success of a ratepayer or similar group in local elections may lead to some changes in the local policies of electorally dominant parties; in order to avoid defeat at the polls, they may make significant modifications in their policies. Indeed, Newton lists rate increases as one of the issues which councillors believe 'could easily tip the often delicate balance between election defeat and victory'. [19] Moreover, as we shall see in Chapter Four, ratepayer protests have had some impact on policy-making at the national level in recent years.

Gyford has observed that 'The distinction between a local party and a local pressure group is hard to make'. [20] This is the case for many ratepayer and similar movements, although there is a sense in which the distinction is not worth making. Many ratepayer groups, of course, never contest elections; they confine themselves to what would conventionally be regarded as pressure group activities such as writing to councillors, holding protest meetings or demonstrations and collecting signatures for petitions. There is some evidence, however, that ratepayer movements are viewed with some distrust by other actors in local political systems and may therefore find it difficult to gain access to decision-makers. In a study of the local amenity movement in Britain, Barker found that some of the respondents ascribed ' "narrow" or sectional motives and interests' [21] to residents' associations and similar bodies. In Banbury, Stacey found that the local Ratepayers' Association 'seemed to feel outside the local power structure and felt that they should aim to get a representative of the Association on all possible committees "so that they would be instrumental in decision-making as opposed to being presented with a *fait accompli*" '. [22] Newton found that in Birmingham, residents' associations were among the categories of organisation viewed by members of the city council 'with anything ranging from scepticism to downright hostility. Such organisations often find it difficult to gain access to elected or appointed officials . . . so they are obliged to use different political tactics'. [23] One possible tactic is to contest local elections.

This monograph does not deal with the Moderate, Progressive, Citizen and other 'concealed Conservative' parties which 'owed their inception to a coming together

4

of Conservatives, Liberals and independents to resist the growth of the Labour Party'. [24] These parties were especially prominent in Central Scotland, the North-East of England and other urban areas where the Labour Party was particularly strong. [25] These movements are excluded from consideration for two reasons. First, there is a reasonably adequate literature on their origins and characteristics. [26] Second, these movements were dealt a particularly heavy blow by the greater politicisation of local government that followed reorganisation. It is true that some of their councillors strongly resisted the importation of national party labels into local politics and that in one or two places these movements survive. However, these survivors are few in number; Glasgow and Edinburgh now have Conservative rather than Progressive councillors and the 'Citizens' no longer dominate Bristol politics. As Gyford puts it, 'the Anti-Socialist caucus is now receding into history as an actor in the local political stage'. [27] This book will concentrate on those aspects of independent local politics which have a continuing relevance to the understanding of local politics in England and Wales.

A principal justification of this study is that independent and ratepayer councillors are significant phenomena in British local politics which require examination if we are to understand the more distinctive aspects of local political behaviour. However, it is also argued that this study has some relevance to the more general concerns of political scientists studying British politics. In particular, it is argued that the study has relevance to three problem areas currently engaging the attention of students of British politics: sporadic interventionism; urban—rural cleavages; and partisan dealignment.

Dowse and Hughes have drawn attention to the neglect of 'sporadic interventionists' by political scientists. [28] Dowse and Hughes are essentially concerned with short-term interventions in politics by people with little previous experience of political activity who have been upset or angered by some aspect of central or local government policy. Ratepayer movements are one form of 'sporadic interventionism' which will be explored in this monograph. Dowse and Hughes suggest that sporadic intervention is likely to increase and the implications of such a development are examined in the monograph.

A number of writers have drawn attention to the presence of urban—rural cleavages in British politics. On the basis of an analysis of aggregate data, Crewe and Payne suggest that 'an urban—rural conflict acts as a weak, secondary but cross-cutting social cleavage to that of class in British electoral behaviour.' [29] Steed has observed that the swings in British general elections from 1970 to October 1974 were 'strikingly different according to the urban—rural dimension'. [30] The persistence of independent politics on local councils in rural areas is another manifestation of this cleavage. The absence of effective party competition in local elections may have some impact on the form and outcome of general election contests in rural areas. There is, however, a general lack of studies of the distinctiveness of rural politics in Britain [31] and it is hoped that Chapter One in particular will go some way towards filling that gap.

The persistence of independent local politics has been matched by an erosion of partisanship in British national politics, what has been termed 'the growing, in fact accelerating, refusal of the electorate to cast a ballot for either of the two governing parties'. [32] Thus, 'the staunch, automatic Labour or Conservative supporter, who could be expected to turn out without fail at every election (local as well as general) and whose outlook on the world was one-sidedly partisan, (has) in the passage of a decade become a member of a small and rapidly dwindling minority group'. [33] One should not, of course, make too ready a connection between the voter who cannot be bothered to increase the size of the Labour majority in an inner city constituency and the voter in a Cornish village who would only vote for an independent in a local government election but quite happily supports a party candidate at each general election. Over ninety per cent of survey respondents are still prepared to give some kind of party identification [34] and, unlike the United States, there is no large body of voters who are prepared to describe themselves as independents. [35]

Nevertheless, both ratepayer and independent councillors do reject conventional party politics, if only at the local level. The distaste for party politics which surfaces in electors' opposition to party politics in local government could, in certain circumstances, be drawn on by populist movements which reject conventional political solutions. In short, it is contended that the phenomena studied in this monograph are a significant aspect of local politics in England and Wales, but they may also have implications for the pattern of national politics as well.

Notes

[1] K. Young, *Local Politics and the Rise of Party*, Leicester University Press, Leicester 1975, p.29.

[2] Throughout this book the term 'independent' is generally used in preference to 'nonpartisan', partly to avoid confusion with the situation in the United States where 'nonpartisan' refers to the exclusion of party labels from ballot papers, partly because independent politics may be partisan.

[3] K. Young, 'Urban Politics: an Overview' in K. Young (ed.), *Essays on the Study of Urban Politics*, Macmillan, London 1975, pp. 185-201, p.193.

[4] K. Young, 'Values in Urban Politics: the Case of "Localism" ', mimeographed paper, Urban and Regional Studies Unit, Centre for Research in the Social Sciences, University of Kent at Canterbury, 1975, p.31.

[5] Young, *Local Politics and the Rise of Party*, op. cit., p.220.

[6] Young, *Values in Urban Politics*, op. cit., p.7.

[7] Ibid., p.7.

[8] *Report of the Committee of Enquiry on Local Government Finance (Layfield Report)*, Cmnd.6453, HMSO, London 1976, p.300.

[9] The thirteen English counties were Cambridge; Cornwall; Devon; Herefordshire; Lincolnshire, Holland; Lincolnshire, Kesteven; Lincolnshire, Lindsey; Rutland; Shropshire; Somerset; Westmorland; Yorkshire (East Riding); Yorkshire (North

Riding). They were the largest single category on Cumberland, Gloucester, Isle of Wight, Oxford and W. Suffolk. The Welsh counties with independent majorities were Anglesey, Caernarvon, Cardigan, Denbigh, Merioneth, Montgomery, Pembroke, Radnor: they were the largest single category on Carmarthern.

[10] D.M. Clark, *Battle For The Counties,* Redrose Publications, Newcastle 1977, p.7.

[11] H. Elcock, 'English Local Government Reformed: The Politics of Humberside', *Public Administration,* vol.53, no.2, Summer 1975, pp. 159-166, p.160.

[12] Gordon, where independents held half of the seats, is counted as independent controlled. The figures for England and Wales are derived from press reports, principally in *The Times;* those from Scotland come from an extremely useful compilation by J.M. Bochel and D.T. Denver, *The Scottish Local Government Elections 1974: Results and Statistics,* Scottish Academic Press, Edinburgh 1975.

[13] J. Stanyer, *Understanding Local Government,* Fontana, London 1976, p.85.

[14] See D. Hill and I. Robinson, *Politics and Local Life: a Study of the Borough and Constituency of Eastleigh,* Social Science Research Council Research Report HR 472, London 1972, p.21 and E. Martin, *The Shearers and the Shorn,* Routledge and Kegan Paul, London 1965, pp.118-9.

[15] T. Brown, M.J.C. Vile and M.F. Whitemore, 'Community Studies and Decision-Taking', *British Journal of Political Science,* vol.2, no.2, April 1972, pp.133-153, p.145.

[16] R.E. Jennings, 'Political Perspectives on Local Government Reorganisation', *Local Government Studies,* October 1975, pp.21-37, p.34.

[17] Elcock, op.cit., p.161.

[18] P. Kantor, 'Elites, Pluralists and Policy Arenas in London: Towards a Comparative Theory of City Policy Formation', *British Journal of Political Science,* vol.6, no.3, July 1976, pp.331-334, p.319.

[19] K. Newton, *Second City Politics,* Oxford University Press, London 1976, p.224.

[20] J. Gyford, *Local Politics in Britain,* Croom Helm, London 1976, p.98.

[21] A. Barker, *The Local Amenity Movement,* Civic Trust, London 1976, p.31.

[22] M. Stacey, E. Batstone, C. Bell and A. Murcott, *Power, Persistence and Change,* Routledge and Kegan Paul, London 1975, p.66.

[23] Newton, op.cit., p.86.

[24] A.J. Beith, 'An Anti-Labour Caucus: The Case of the Northumberland Voters' Association', *Policy and Politics,* vol.2, no.2, 1974, pp.153-165, p.153.

[25] See Young, *Rise of Party,* op.cit., p.135.

[26] Principally Young, ibid.; Beith, op.cit.; J.H. Robbins, 'The Conservative Intervention in Doncaster Borough Politics', *British Journal of Political Science,* vol.2, no.4, October 1972, pp.510-512. There are also references to such movements in a number of the studies of particular communities produced in recent years: see, for example, W. Hampton, *Democracy and Community: a Study of Politics in Sheffield,* Oxford University Press, London 1970, p.63.

[27] Gyford, op.cit., p.100.

[28] R.E. Dowse and J. Hughes, 'Sporadic Interventionists', *Political Studies*, vol.25, no.1, March 1977, pp.84-92.

[29] I. Crewe and C. Payne, 'Another Game With Nature: An Ecological Regression Model of the British Two-Party Vote Ratio in 1970', *British Journal of Political Science*, vol.6, no.1, January 1976, pp.43-81, p.67.

[30] M. Steed, 'The Results Analysed' in D. Butler and D. Kavanagh, *The British General Election of October 1974*, Macmillan, London 1975, pp.330-356, p.350.

[31] A distinguished exception is P. Madgwick, *The Politics of Rural Wales*, Hutchinson, London 1973.

[32] I. Crewe, B. Särlvik and J. Alt, 'Partisan Dealignment in Britain 1964-1974', *British Journal of Political Science*, vol.7, no.2, April 1977, pp.129-190, p.129.

[33] Ibid., p.142.

[34] Ibid., p.144.

[35] Ibid., p.184.

1　Independent politics

This chapter examines the various patterns of politics which develop on councils that have a majority or a substantial number of councillors elected without a party label. Councils controlled by independents are a rural phenomenon. Hjellum found in Norway [1] that the resistance to party politicisation was at its greatest in the least urbanised communities and this pattern is replicated in Britain. In England and Wales, there is only a scattering of independents on the metropolitan district councils. In the non-metropolitan districts, the mean population density of councils controlled by independents in 1976 was 0.72 persons per hectare; the most densely populated district controlled by independents had only 1.78 persons per hectare.

Table 1.1

Independent politics and rurality in England and Wales, 1976

Non-metropolitan districts

Percentage of seats held by independents in 1976	Persons per hectare		
	less than 0.95	0.95–1.94	over 1.95
less than 25%	13.4% (9)	40.3% (27)	94.0% (187)
25%–49%	13.4% (9)	38.8% (26)	6.0% (12)
Over 50%	73.1% (49)	20.9% (14)	0.0% (0)
N = 333	99.9% (67)	100% (67)	100% (199)

A similar pattern may be observed in Scotland:

Table 1.2

Independent politics and rurality in Scotland, 1974

District councils

Percentage of seats held by independents in 1974	Persons per hectare		
	less than 0.45	0.45–5.0	over 5.0
less than 25%	4.2% (1)	82.4% (14)	91.7% (11)
25%–49%	16.7% (4)	11:8% (2)	8.3% (1)
Over 50%	79.2% (19)	5.9% (1)	0.0% (1)
	100.1% (24)	100.1% (17)	100% (12)

District councils controlled by independents tend to be in the remoter rural areas. For example, over half (33) of the sixty-three district councils controlled by independents in England and Wales in 1976 were in seven western counties: Cornwall, Devon, Salop, Hereford & Worcester, Powys, Gwynedd and Dyfed. Conversely, thirty-eight of the fifty-one non-metropolitan districts with population densities below 1.75 persons per hectare which were *not* controlled by independents were in the South-East of England. East Anglia and the Midlands. [2]

9

Why do patterns of independent politics tend to persist in the remoter rural areas? Two complementary approaches may be adopted to this problem. One approaches stresses the importance of local social structures and political cultures; the other emphasises the role of the political parties in politicising the remoter rural areas. A social structural explanation would point to the relative stability of the population in such areas, enabling a candidate to be known personally to a large number of voters. A suspicion of 'outsiders' may lead voters to attach more importance to length of residence and local connections than to party affiliations. Thus, one has a highly 'localist' political culture which represents a substantial barrier to national political influences in local politics.

The other approach considers the costs and benefits of contesting elections in a rural area from the viewpoint of a political party. The costs of contesting an election are higher in a rural area than an urban area; for example, if a canvass is to be organised, there is a greater distance to be covered, quite apart from the difficulty of actually locating properties in a rural area. As far as benefits are concerned, county councils discharge the more important functions (e.g., education) in non-metropolitan areas and there is thus an incentive for the party to concentrate its efforts at that level. Moreover, it may be suggested that more prestige accrues to a party that wins a metropolitan district or even a non-metropolitan district serving a well-known city (e.g., Oxford) than to a party that wins control of a district council of the 'North Barsetshire' type serving some amorphous slice of a remote rural county.

When the factors discussed above are combined with the resistance of electors to party candidates, [3] it is not surprising that political parties (especially the Conservatives) often fear that by contesting seats held by independents in rural areas, they may simply allow a candidate from an opposition party to win. However, the incentive to contest is greater in districts forming part of marginal Parliamentary seats; for example, Liberal intervention in local elections in the Carrick and Restormel districts in Cornwall may be related to the marginality of the Truro and North Cornwall constituencies. Moreover, the development of Nationalism in Scotland and Wales may hasten the erosion of independent politics, although the Nationalists have often been reluctant to intervene in local elections in independent areas even in constituencies which they hold or are close to winning. Present indications are that independent politics is losing most ground in relatively more urbanised areas; the fourteen district councils lost by independents in England in the 1976 elections had a mean population density of 1.73 persons per hectare, compared with 0.72 for the authorities remaining in independent control. The resistance to party politics in local government in the remoter rural areas of western England and Wales seems to remain relatively strong.

Independent councillors were dealt a heavy blow by local government reorganisation. In part, this was because independent councils were merged with councils with a tradition of party political activity. The spread of party politics on the reorganised councils was also 'the outcome of an explicit Conservative policy of encouraging former Independents of Conservative leaning to stand under the party label or else face an official Conservative opponent'. [4] The Labour Party also attempted to increase its penetration in rural areas, although its exhortations to its members in areas such as Devon to fight in the hills and 'on the beaches' carried a somewhat hollow ring.

Thus, many areas which had formerly been represented only by independent councillors found themselves politicised as a consequence of local government reorganisation. Similarly, in the 1976 district council elections there were one or two cases of the 'sudden death' of an independent council in the face of a determined onslaught by the local Conservative Party. For example, the Conservatives 'gained' 31 seats from independents to take control of East Devon Council in 1976. In fact, of course, the turnover of councillors was less dramatic than the figure quoted implies; many independents either underwent a 'label change' to re-emerge as Conservatives or stood down in the face of the concerted onslaught by a formidable local Conservative machine.

In many areas, however, the process has been one of a gradual erosion of independent strength. For example, consider the 'Central' District Council which was 'gained' by the Conservatives from independents in 1976 and forms the basis for one of the case studies examined later in the chapter. The 'Central' District was formed from a non-county borough, where candidates stood under political labels, and four rural districts which had always been governed by independents. The first district council elections held in 1973 produced what was, at least superficially, an extremely complex pattern of contests. 10 Independents and 6 Conservatives were returned unopposed. 7 Independents were returned in straight 'fights' with Labour and another 7 were returned in contests against other Independents. 6 Conservatives were elected in straight 'fights' with Independents and another 5 were elected against opposition only from the Liberals. 2 Independents defeated Conservative opponents and 1 fought off a Conservative and Labour challenge. 1 Conservative was opposed by Independent and Liberal challengers and 1 Independent defeated Liberal opposition. One three-seat ward returned a Liberal, Conservative and Independent with a Conservative and a Labour candidate being unsuccessful. 4 other Liberals were returned and 1 Labour candidate sneaked in past Independent opposition. Thus, overall, the council contained 28 Independents, 20 Conservatives, 5 Liberals and 1 Labour representative. Perhaps the most significant statistic is that only nine wards (out of 36) saw contests between Conservative and Independent candidates. Three of these were multi-member wards which returned both Conservative and Independent councillors. Thus, only six wards saw direct clashes between the Conservatives and Independents. Recalling one of these contests, a councillor who was interviewed as part of this study remarked, 'The sitting member for (village) who was a Liberal put up in protest because I was a Conservative and not standing as an Independent'.

Relations between the Conservative and Independent 'groups' on the council were generally harmonious between 1973 and 1976, except for one dispute over the allocation of committee chairmanships. The council returned in 1976 consisted of 26 Conservatives, 21 Independents, 4 Liberals and 3 Ratepayers. Thus the

Conservatives became the largest 'group' and effectively gained control; the way in which they did this illustrates the confused character of electoral politics in areas which are in a transitional stage from being entirely nonpartisan to entirely party political. The Conservatives made 8 gains from Independents (and 2 from Liberals); six of the gains from Independents were due to councillors changing their electoral labels. Rather more surprisingly, as well as gaining one seat from the Labour Party and one from the Liberals, the Independents managed to take two seats from the Conservatives; in one ward, where the Conservatives had held one seat, they did not put forward any candidates and the Independents made a net gain of one. Similarly, the Conservatives failed to nominate in another ward where they had held one seat. [5] On this occasion, there were direct clashes between Conservatives and Independents in only three wards.

It is clear from the interviews that were conducted in 1977 with the members of this council that the Conservatives had attempted to persuade their supporters to stand under the party banner, but that they were unwilling to put up candidates against known Conservatives who stood as Independents. Clearly, the decision to change from Independent to Conservative was a difficult one for many councillors. For example, one respondent commented, 'I had quite a tussle as to what to do . . . I am a Conservative, although I don't like party politics in local government . . . I was in a dilemma for quite a while'. On the other hand, another respondent who was a Conservative in national politics and claimed to have defeated a Labour sympathiser standing as an Independent in 1973, declared his determination to remain an Independent: 'No one's going to tell me how I vote or what I do'.

On a council like 'Central', whether a ward has a Conservative or Independent representative depends very much on the inclination of the serving councillor, provided that he is not suspected of being a covert radical. However, the bargaining position of Independents becomes much weaker as their numbers reduce in relation to the preponderant party group. There is a wide range of rewards and sanctions which a controlling party group can use to persuade an independent to accept the party ticket. For example, in their study of Cheshire, Lee et al. note that in their preparations for the 1970 county elections, 'the Conservative group wished to run a candidate in every county division but feared such tactics might lead to Labour victories wherever a popular Independent split the Conservative vote'. [6] However, some Independents stood down or were persuaded to stand as Conservatives and in the run-up to the 1973 elections the Conservatives attempted to persuade the nine Independents to accept nomination as Conservatives; 'it was pointed out privately to them that the possibility of opposition from a party candidate could not be ruled out'. [7] After reorganisation 'The small group of Independents decided informally to support the Conservatives. In exchange they received important patronage positions'. [8]

The extent to which the Conservative Party will seek to replace Independents by official party nominees will depend on a number of factors. In a situation where the Conservative Party is strong in a locality, there is little risk that contesting independent seats will let in Liberal or Labour representatives. On the other hand, given that most of the councillors in such an area will probably be sympathetic to Conservative principles, there is little incentive to embark on an electoral strategy of eradicating independents which might be costly in terms of effort and money and lead to ill-feeling among Conservatives. However, if the political situation in either the constituency or on the council changes, the incentives to contest independent wards became greater. If a constituency becomes more marginal (for example, as the result of a Liberal or Nationalist upsurge), contesting local elections can help to keep the party machine well oiled and give a useful boost to party morale. Similarly, an upsurge in representation from other parties on the council may lead the Conservatives to take a greater interest in local elections. For example, in Cheshire the 1964 elections in which the Conservatives lost eight seats to Labour 'had for the first time since the mid-1930s made the group conscious of its dependence on the votes of Independents, if it were obliged to assemble a majority'. [9] A change of local party leader may also make a difference; under new leadership, the Cheshire Conservative group 'began to adopt a much more aggressive posture in its approach to electioneering'. [10]

It should not be assumed, however, that Conservative interventions in local politics in areas with a preponderance of independent representation are governed solely by the marginality or otherwise of the constituency and local political situation. A well-organised Conservative Party in a relatively safe seat (e.g., the East Devon council in the Honiton constituency) may simply decide that the time has come for its strength to be reflected more clearly in terms of local political representation. Equally, Conservatives in a relatively marginal constituency may decide not to contest local elections. For example, the 'Westward' council discussed later in the chapter is located in a constituency where the Liberal challenge has to be taken seriously, but the Conservatives have not contested the district council elections (although the Labour Party have fought some seats and managed to elect a councillor). The official Conservative explanation is that no nominations have been put forward by their branches. One can only speculate about their reasons for failing to nominate, but it may be that they recognise that a political intervention directed against established local councillors might not be popular with the electorate. In the last report, much will depend on local party leaders' perceptions of the attitudes of the electorate towards party politics in local government. In some cases, they may be misled into thinking that the intensity of feeling of many independent councillors on this subject is shared by the electorate, although there is certainly evidence that the electorate find party politics in local government distasteful. [11] Moreover, it must be stressed that these choices by party leaders must be viewed in the context of the greater costs and less tangible benefits of intervention in local elections in rural areas.

The recruitment of independent councillors

One of the functions of a political party is to select candidates for public office. In local government, a political party may actively encourage particular individuals who are regarded as potentially good councillors to offer their services. How do candidates emerge in the absence of political parties performing this kind of function?

In answering this question, and others posed later in the chapter, considerable use will be made of data gathered in a study of two English non-metropolitan district councils, called here 'Central' and 'Westward'. The 'Central' District Council serves an area of some 250,000 acres with a population of around 100,000 in the English Midlands. As has already been pointed out, it was controlled by independents from 1973 to 1976 when the Conservatives became the largest group. The 'Westward' District Council serves an area of some 75,000 acres with a population of around 50,000 in the West of England. In 1976 its political composition was Independents 39, Labour 1. Thirteen councillors were interviewed from each council; in each case, the Chairman, Vice-Chairman and the chairman of the major programme committees were interviewed, the balance being made up of councillors selected at random. [12] In addition, observation at the meetings of the two councils made an important contribution to the study.

Although both the areas studied are rural in the sense that they are not densely populated and that agriculture makes a substantial contribution to the local economy, they differ in a number of significant ways. Most importantly, apart from the difference of size, the 'Central' District is more prosperous. This difference is reflected in a number of statistics. For example, unemployment in 'Central' was below the national average at the time of the study; in 'Westward' it was substantially above the national average. In 'Westward', 48 per cent of households do not have access to a car; in 'Central' the corresponding figure is 30 per cent. In 'Westward' the rateable value per head is £102; in 'Central' it is £137. 'Westward' is located in a county in which the modal size of agricultural holding is between 50 and 99 acres; in the county in which 'Central' is located, the modal size is between 100 and 299 acres. Fewer households in 'Westward' (80 per cent compared with 90 per cent in 'Central') have exclusive use of hot water, a fixed bath and an inside w.c. One further difference between the areas, which does not relate to their relative prosperity, is that the 'Central' District was formed from a merger of one non-county borough and four rural districts, whereas 'Westward' brought together two non-county boroughs, one urban district and one rural district. Only 21 per cent of the population of 'Central' is located in the largest town and 'administrative capital'; the corresponding figure in 'Westward' is 38 per cent (although the old non-county borough area does include a large rural tract). Both districts are located in Conservative constituencies, although the Conservative share of the poll in the October 1974 general election was somewhat higher in 'Central' than in 'Westward'. [13]

In order to explore the process of recruitment to an independent council in a rural area (most of the 'Central' respondents were either independents or had originally been elected as independents), respondents were asked why they had originally become councillors. Their replies are tabulated below (some respondents mentioned more than one reason):

Table 1.2
Reasons for becoming a councillor

	'Central'	'Westward'	Total
Personal reasons			
Asked to stand	6	2	8
Succeeded father/family tradition	1	5	6
Desire to serve community	–	3	3
Too many 'outsiders' on council	–	2	2
Retirement	1	1	2
Extension of occupational role	1	–	1
Encouraged by organisation	–	1	1
Persuaded by workmates	–	1	1
Need for women members	–	1	1
Extension of town council work	1	–	1
Reasons related to performance of council			
Dissatisfaction with calibre/ performance of serving councillors	2	5	7
Dissatisfaction with handling of specific issues	1	2	3

Twenty-seven respondents gave personal reasons for originally seeking election, as against thirteen who gave performance-related reasons. In particular, dissatisfaction over policy or the handling of a particular issue was a rare motivation for seeking election; more usually, respondents who gave 'performance-related' reasons simply had a low opinion of the serving councillors:

> I always thought the (old) council were men rather affected by senile decay. I could reason as well as they if not better.

In 'Central', 'being asked' was the single most important reason for standing:

> There was a vacancy for the Rural District Council and I was approached by various people in the village because they didn't seem to have a candidate. Retiring member came and asked me to.

In 'Westward', 'family tradition' was the most important reason for standing:

> My father was a member all his time and he took on from his father and I followed on.

Thus in 'Central', which is nearer the large conurbations than 'Westward', the process of candidate recruitment is more like that found in fully politicised areas; candidates do not emerge naturally from the local social structure, they have to be sought out and persuaded to stand. In 'Westward', the involvement in community life of certain families who have farmed or run small businesses for several generations is accepted as normal and welcome. [14] As one respondent put it:

> My family has been in the area since my great-grandfather's time. I felt that I had a responsibility to do something for the area in return for what we have received out of it. My grandfather was a county councillor and a district councillor in his time. I felt that I should continue to preserve our heritage and give something back.

Deciding to stand is, of course, only one part of the process of recruitment. The absence of party politics does not mean that elections are not keenly contested; rather the contrary (the extreme example is the island of St. Agnes, the most southerly and westerly electoral district in Britain, where one hundred per cent of the electorate turned out to select two councillors from three candidates in the 1976 Isles of Scilly Council elections). 'Westward' has a rather more vigorous electoral tradition than 'Central'; in the original district council elections in 1973, every ward was contested in 'Westward', whereas there was no contest in fourteen of the 'Central' wards. In 1976, eight of the eleven 'Westward' wards were contested; as in 1973, turnout approached seventy per cent in the more rural wards. In 'Central', eighteen out of the thirty-six wards were not contested. The majority of the contests in 'Central' in 1976 were in the small towns and large villages; there were few contests in the wards made up of small villages. Ranked in terms of density of population, there were contests in fifteen of the first sixteen wards; there were only three contests in the other twenty wards.

Elections in nonpartisan localities

What forces shape the outcome of elections fought between independent candidates? A sixfold categorisation of types of electoral conflict is set out below in an attempt to provide a framework within which this question can be answered:

1. One pattern of electoral behaviour is where a social elite (or its nominees) are returned without contest at successive elections. Dyer's account of county politics in Kincardineshire shows that 'there have been but thirty-three contested elections in the county out of a possible two hundred and seventy-three since 1929'. [15] In 1970, 66.7 per cent of the county councillors were landowners. However, although this type of independent politics has been important in the past (particularly on rural county councils), it is of little continuing importance today. For example, in 'Westward' a member of a prominent local landowning family stood in the 1973 district council elections announcing in an advertisement in the local paper, 'Mr XYZ is standing for election in the Great Rural Area of (name of town)'. He was not elected (although he polled a respectable vote).

2. A variant of the first category is 'succession politics' in which sons (not daughters) succeed fathers, grandfathers, uncles or other relatives; the difference from the first category is that the candidates are not drawn from particularly

wealthy families but share a similar life style to the people they seek to represent. As has already been pointed out, 'succession politics' is of some importance in a remoter rural area like 'Westward', although succeeding one's father does not guarantee electoral success. For example, one candidate for 'Westward' in 1973 announced: 'My father has served as a Parish Councillor for 41 years and on the Rural District for 27 years and now feels that the time has come for him to retire from public service. I would very much like to carry on in his place as my views are very much the same as his.' He was defeated. Certainly, candidates who stand in rural areas are anxious to reassure voters of the impeccability of their local credentials: 'I have what some people consider to be a foreign sounding name, so I must explain that I have lived in this area all my life.'

3. Particularly since reorganisation, a number of rural electoral divisions contain two (or more) villages of roughly equivalent size. The election can then become a contest between candidates from different villages. One of the most ingenious ploys observed by the author in this kind of situation was in a ward with two villages of equal size. The winning candidate in a three-cornered contest emphasised that although she came from one village, her husband was a native of the other village. The importance of maintaining an electoral balance between different communities can become an issue when boundaries are redrawn. For example, in 'Westward', ninety-six per cent of the electorate in one parish signed a petition against their being joined to a small town in a reorganisation of electoral boundaries. It was argued, '(The parish) is one of five parishes in the ward, all of comparable electoral size and therefore able to compete fairly in a poll to provide a district councillor. Joined to the single parish ward of (the town), the parish will have less than one-sixth of the electoral numbers of (the town) and, in practice, its electors would be virtually disenfranchised in any future district council election.'

4. In his study of Kincardineshire, Dyer argues that 'elections are something of a personality contest in which the candidate with the most friends and neighbours wins'. [16] 'Friends and neighbours' voting of this type can be important in small electoral divisions, although it is unlikely to give a candidate a sufficient electoral base in the larger divisions which have been formed since reorganisation. However, persons in certain 'political occupations' [17] (e.g., vicars, veterinary surgeons, auctioneers) may have a sufficiently wide range of contacts to garner large numbers of votes from electors who know them personally.

5. In some circumstances, 'sponsoring groups' may endorse candidates. These are local organisations (chambers of commerce, ratepayers associations, hoteliers associations etc.) who encourage candidates to stand and announce their public support for the candidates but do not finance their campaigns. When a local organisation overtly identifies itself with a particular group of candidates, it may seem difficult to distinguish the sponsoring group from the ordinary political party, apart from the fact that sponsoring groups are not organised on a national basis (or, at least, only on a confederal basis). In fact, the distinction is not an easy one to make, for they do perform similar functions (the selection and promotion of candidates) in rather different political contexts. One difference between the political

party and the sponsoring group is to be found in the character of the relationship between the councillor and the group which supported his electoral campaign. However, this is a difference of degree rather than of kind. Although the councillor supported by a sponsoring group is not subject to the discipline of any party group system once he has been elected and has only an informal relationship with his sponsors, not all political party councillors find themselves working within a framework of strict group discipline or a structure of strict accountability to the local party. All one can say is that sponsoring groups do not have any formal disciplinary system, and that political parties may have, and even where they do they will not necessarily adhere to it very strictly. In fact, the informal social pressures which can be exerted by a chamber of commerce in a small town on one of its members who is a councillor may be just as considerable as the pressure which can be exerted by a political party on one of its councillors. Political parties and sponsoring groups may be arrayed on a continuum of formality – informality in disciplinary and accountability arrangements, but the behavioural realities may differ less than the formal procedures. If one wishes to make an arbitrary distinction between a political party and a sponsoring group, it may be fruitful to focus on the question of finance. One of the major functions of political parties is to raise funds which may be used to support the electoral campaigns of adopted candidates. Sponsoring groups limit their activity to *endorsing* the candidate; any campaign expenditure is a matter for the candidate himself. Political parties and sponsoring groups may thus be differentiated in terms of the arrangements which are made for financing candidates. The emergence of sponsoring groups in a nonpartisan district may be one of the first signs of an impending transition from a nonpartisan to a partisan system.

6. In some instances, there may be genuine policy conflicts between independent candidates. For example, one candidate may place greater emphasis on economy in local government than his opponents. Candidates may stand on a particular controversial issue. For example, voters in one ward in 'Westward' in 1973 were exhorted to vote for 'X and Y, your staunch anti-sewage pipeline candidates'. On the whole, however, the election campaigns of independent candidates are rarely built around particular issues. One successful candidate in 'Westward' simply informed electors in an advertisement in the local paper: 'Thanks electors for past support. I trust you will continue your valued support. I will do my best, if re-elected, to merit your support as I have always tried to do.'

Councillors in 'Central' and 'Westward' were asked to account for their electoral success, the question posed being 'What sorts of factors or events have exercised the most influence over the results of the elections you have contested?' Newton has argued that 'the term "local election" is something of a misnomer, for there is very little that is local about them . . . They are determined overwhelmingly by national political considerations. Local elections are a sort of annual general election'. [18] This may be so in cities like Birmingham, but it does not apply to areas where only a minority of candidates have political labels. Seventy per cent of Newton's Birmingham respondents said that national factors were among the

18

most important influences on elections; none of the 'Westward' and 'Central' respondents mentioned national factors as an element in their success and only four mentioned the effectiveness of their party organisations:

Table 1.4

Councillors' explanations of their electoral success

	'Central'	'Westward'	Total
Well known	4	5	9
Record of service	1	6	7
Local person/length of residence	3	3	6
Effectiveness of party organisation/party affiliation	2	2	4
Extensive canvass	3	–	3
Wife/parent/family well known	2	1	3
Never opposed	2	–	2
Particular issue(s)	1	1	2
Outspoken personality	1	1	2

Reasons mentioned once: opposition to party politics; local government experience; nominated by retiring councillor; woman; Celtic nationality.

On the whole, then, it would seem that a candidate who has lived in the area for a long time and is an experienced and well-known councillor has the greatest chance of success. This is not, of course, in any sense an 'iron law'. One councillor had been elected after living in 'Westward' for less than a year — but he was in a 'political occupation' and nominated by a retiring councillor.

The elections in 'Central' in 1973 and 1976 have been discussed earlier in the chapter. 'Westward' offers an example of a district where party labels rarely appear. There were two Labour candidates in 1973, one of whom was elected; he was returned unopposed in 1976 (a 'Christian Socialist' also stood in 1976). One Liberal stood in 1973, but was returned as an independent in 1976. 'Sponsoring groups' played a relatively small part; two successful candidates in 1976 had the support of ratepayers' associations.

Conflict over policy seemed to affect the result of the election in only one of the wards. This was in the ward with the highest turnout (a rural ward) where the Chairman of the Council attempted to defend the council against what he saw as 'ill-informed and often blatantly inaccurate comment, which betrays an appalling lack of knowledge of the scope and complexity of current District Council administration'. In spite of his defence of the Council's policies (particularly expenditure on recreational facilities in rural areas), he finished bottom of the poll, his seat being taken by the local county councillor who promised to oppose 'colossal expenditure' and 'extravagance'. As far as the other two rural wards were concerned, in one the three retiring members were re-elected, one from each of the main settlements. The candidate who came fourth was from the largest village in the ward. In the other rural ward, the three members returned were each from different villages; a retiring councillor who was unable to campaign because of illness was defeated. There is some evidence that (particularly in the small towns), candidates who emphasised the need to restrain council spending did rather better than those who took a different stance (two candidates who, in effect, called for more spending to tackle local problems fared particularly badly). The average vote obtained by five candidates who emphasised the need to curb spending (1,056) was well above the average for all candidates (757).

It might seem that independent councils would enjoy electoral patterns of great stability with a low turnover of councillors. However, in fact, one-third of the membership of the 'Central' and 'Westward' councils was replaced in the 1976 elections. Fifteen of these replacements were due to members retiring, but sixteen serving councillors were defeated, including the Chairman and Vice-Chairman of 'Westward' and the Chairman-elect of 'Central'. As has been pointed out, the Chairman of 'Westward' was defeated after an intensely fought campaign which produced a poll of just under 70 per cent. One councillor commented in relation to this and other campaigns, 'The council is something of an Aunt Sally. New members can always get in on a protest vote.'

Decision-making on independent councils

The recruitment of councillors is an interesting and important topic in itself, but the study of local politics should not stop short at the returning officer's declaration of the poll. Councillors are of general interest because they take decisions; in particular, district councils are taking important decisions in the areas of housing and planning. The absence of party groups on independent councils leaves something of a vacuum in the decision-making process. The role which such a group may play in the decision-making process on a council has been described by Spencer in his account of 'Aberton', an industrial town in the north of England with a Labour controlled council. [19] The Labour group was involved 'in two sorts of activity: screening the decisions already made in the various committees before they were ratified by the council on the one hand; and arriving at an agreed group policy towards certain more general issues on the other'. [20] Spencer emphasises, 'There could never be any question as to the prime allegiance of any member of the group'. [21] If a committee member disagreed with his Labour colleagues, 'the correct place to argue his case was in the meetings of the Labour group and not in the committee or council. If he failed to persuade them to change their views then he was obliged to withhold his opposition or face disciplinary action . . . leaving him in political isolation.' [22]

Of the questions asked of 'Central' and 'Westward' councillors, the one that produced the most emphatic responses was 'What part, if any, should party politics play in local government?' Many councillors simply answered 'None' or 'None whatsoever'. Only three of the twenty-six councillors interviewed thought that there was a place for party politics in local government, although four councillors thought that its spread was regrettably inevitable. However, the majority of councillors emphasised that, whatever their personal views on national politics, these played no part in their decisions on local matters:

> I speak as a Liberal, we also have Conservatives, we don't make decisions along party lines in these parts, we do try to come to a position of agreement dealing with the facts as they present themselves. I don't ever vote politically, I have voted on issues disloyal to the Red Flag, I have voted against it.

Party politics plays a more overt role in the 'Central' District Council, where there is a Conservative group and an Independent 'group', although the latter meets only before the annual general meeting. However, this has to be set against the greater political homogeneity of the 'Central' council (one respondent estimated that 50 out of its 54 councillors were Conservatives in national politics), whereas the 'Westward' council seemed to be more heterogeneous in terms of the national political affiliation of its members. [23] In both districts the main division in national politics is the Conservative–Liberal one, but Liberalism appears to have deeper social roots in Methodism in 'Westward'. Methodist chapels are to be found along the remotest lanes and in the most isolated hamlets, and although many of these are now either derelict or have only occasional services, Methodism is still enough of a force for five hundred people to turn out for the funeral of a noted local preacher in 1976.

The Conservative group appears to play a very limited role in the decision-making process on the 'Central' council. One respondent from 'Central' commented: 'There is very little party politics in our district . . . perhaps in choosing chairmen it's important.' In fact, the allocation of chairmanships is the only issue that ever seems to have led to any friction (and then only once) between Independents and Conservatives on the council. At present, all but one of the major committee chairmanships are held by the Conservatives, who also have a majority on the Policy & Resources Committee. Committee memberships are allocated in accordance with geographical criteria: councillors caucus into four 'geographical' groups, largely based on the pre-reorganisation boundaries. Each group has a number of seats on each committee allocated to it in accordance with its size and a complex permutation system taking account of the geographical origins of the Chairman of the Council and the Chairman of Policy and Resources. Respondents commented only one issue had ever aroused any political controversy on the council (the Community Land Act). Voting figures at council meetings do not reflect 'party' divisions. For example, at a council meeting in 1976 there was a roll-call vote on a motion opposing the appointment of an Assistant to the Chief Executive. If party affiliations were important, one would expect them to manifest themselves in a vote of this kind, but in fact 8 Conservatives voted for the motion and 13 against; the Independents split 6-14; and even the small Liberal group was not unanimous (the two Ratepayer councillors present both voted the same way).

'Westward', of course, has only one official party representative. As one respondent commented, 'Westward is one of the most independent of Councils and party politics very rarely enter into our deliberations. Our decisions are made according to the need in hand and what is deemed best for 'Westward' is always political but very rarely party political.'

It is, of course, possible for a nonpartisan electoral process to be combined with the existence of covert or overt groupings on the council. Beith uses the term 'caucus parties' to describe organisations of 'councillors . . . on a single local authority with no external organisation'. [24] One of the few candidates who stood in 'Westward' elections under a party label justified his breach of local political norms in the following terms in a local newspaper: 'Man is a political animal and even in our chamber of Independents, it does not prevent groups of members with political leanings getting together as a block behind or against a particular motion before any committee with a view to influencing the final decision of the full council.'

In fact, there are some indications that informal groupings may exist on the Westward District Council. An analysis of seven roll-call votes showed that three 'groups' of members voted together. First, three former members of the largest of the old non-county boroughs voted together; in particular, they voted against a motion to cut the Council's budget for a particular item by £30,000 which was carried by one vote. Next, there were five councillors who (when they were present) voted the same way as the then Liberal Parliamentary candidate who was a member of the council. Last, the most vociferous critic of spending on the council attracted consistent support from two other councillors on expenditure issues.

However, one should not make too much of these apparent voting patterns. The councillors who vote together in this way do not sit together in council meetings and there is certainly no evidence that they meet together. Indeed, one point that was stressed very strongly by the councillors in their interviews was their belief in individual judgement, in assessing a problem on its merits in the light of local conditions. This was, for them, an essential part of their commitment to a philosophy of independence in local politics. In order to understand how such councillors act without party guidance, one has to consider their individual perceptions of their roles as councillors.

Role perceptions of councillors

There has been an increasing interest in recent years in the role perceptions of councillors — how they see their job — stemming from a more general interest in the behaviour of legislatures of all kinds. [25] In particular, there has been an interest in whether councillors see themselves as 'trustees', 'delegates' or 'politicos'. As Newton points out, 'the trustee regards himself as a relatively free and independent agent who is elected to follow his own conscience, exercise his own judgement, and act according to his own assessment of the situation. In contrast, the delegate chooses to give greater weight to the wishes and views of the electorate . . . The third type, the politico, tries to fuse or combine these two. [26] The distinction may be made clearer by quoting some of the responses of councillors to the question, 'It is often said that there are two main theories of political representation. The first says that the representative should be the voice of the people and should act as they want him to. The second says that the representative should exercise his own judgement and act according to his own conscience and his own assessment of the situation. Which do you agree with most?' Among the replies were:

> You've got to decide sometimes that if the people want something very strongly, you vote against your conscience. *(Delegate)*
> Very definitely the second. I am elected as a representative and not as a delegate. *(Trustee)*
> Should be a combination of both in this, as a councillor I go round and talk to people, the one thing I don't do is take directives. You have to talk to people and get their opinions, at times you have to act contrary to the pressures you get, you find that you have to follow your own conscience, but I don't think that a councillor should go entirely on his own judgement and conscience, he then becomes a bit of a despot . . . you've got to reason out a thing yourself, find out what the people think and form a judgement bearing in mind what they say to you. *(Politico)*

Not surprisingly, the modal category was that of trustee (14) with only two councillors being classified as delegates and 10 as politicos. As one councillor pointed out. 'The first one (delegate) is political, the second one (trustee) is independent'. The proportion of delegates was far smaller than that found in Newton's Birmingham study (8 per cent compared with 26 per cent). One point that was stressed by a number of councillors was that they were often able to win the electorate round to their point of view, but that even if they couldn't, the electorate respected and would vote for a man who was prepared to speak out and defend his point of view. As one councillor remarked, 'Nobody likes a yes man. There are always two bodies of opinion, you sometimes have to take a minority view. As long as you can state your case, you get respected a damn sight more'.

Recent studies have paid some attention to what are termed the 'areal roles' of councillors and respondents were asked, 'Speaking for yourself, do you think your main job as a councillor is (predominantly) to represent the people in your ward or to govern the district as a whole?' The results are not greatly out of line with those reported by Newton for Birmingham, with 12 respondents choosing the district, 12 the ward and two a mixture of both. Fewer respondents chose this last option than in Birmingham, but this may have something to do with the way in which the questionnaire was administered (or the replies coded) rather than any real difference of outlook.

The questionnaire was also used to explore the extent to which councillors preferred dealing with broad policy questions or individual problems. Respondents were asked, 'Which of these two aspects of council work do you prefer: making broad policy decisions or dealing with the problems of individuals?' Fourteen preferred the individual problems, seven preferred policy and five liked both. It is clear that many councillors gained considerable personal satisfaction from dealing with individual problems:

> I suppose basically I prefer individual problems. I get a lot of pleasure from those — you get an end product which you do not always get with a policy.
> Dealing with the problems of individuals provides more immediate satisfaction in that one feels that one is actually helping people in situations which can be readily understood, whereas the other can be unpalatable, largely because decisions are often governed by criteria outside one's control.

A further distinction in the literature on the role orientations of elected representative is between 'facilitators', 'neutrals' and 'resisters' according to the representative's attitude towards and knowledge of pressure groups. Following Newton, the use of the term 'pressure group' was avoided in the questionnaire and respondents were asked, 'There are two views about the involvement of voluntary organisations and clubs in the work of the district council. The first says that in trying to influence council decisions they interfere with the work of council members who are the democratically elected representatives of the people. The second says that groups can help in the democratic running of a council. Which do you agree with?'

21 of the 26 respondents were classified as 'facilitators'. This figure of 81 per cent corresponds very closely with the figure of 82 per cent noted by Newton in Birmingham. [27] Of course, it should be stressed that the 'facilitators' emphasised the importance of carefully sifting any advice or information received from pressure groups:

> They have the right to have their views heard, but not the divine right of taking decisions.
> You should listen to a lot of groups and make your own mind up. Sometimes you get some really good ideas, other times you get proper old women's tales.

Five of the facilitators differentiated in their answers between different *types* of group. They thought that some organisations had a more positive contribution to make to the work of the council than others:

> This depends entirely on the actual group. I can't say that I would be influenced by all groups, but I would weigh up the group and the responsibility of the group and the particular matter that they were pressing before deciding whether they would influence me or not. We must listen to people who have an interest in some area which is of benefit to the community as a whole, I object to what I call pure pressure groups when you have threats issued by certain organisations in order to achieve a position which you believe is unachievable.

Four respondents singled out ratepayers' associations as examples of the type of group they were less likely to listen to. Newton noted in Birmingham that such associations were viewed 'with anything ranging from scepticism to downright hostility'. [28] As one of our respondents put it:

> The Ratepayers Association at (X) has six or seven at its annual general meeting, you get a few diehards come along and they say that they represent three hundred people, but the voice of that meeting is really only the voice of the six people there.

Only four respondents were classified as 'resisters' (one was 'neutral'):

> You tend to form friendships within these groups and these friendships can be rather embarrassing. When you have to make a decision on something you should be detached from that sort of body.

However, the general consensus of opinion seemed to be that groups could often make a useful contribution to the work of the council and that (particularly since reorganisation) they offered one means of keeping in touch with the public. Moreover, as one councillor commented, 'I would rather have the interest groups identifiable rather than covert.' On the other hand, councillors were aware that groups often represented the views of a vocal minority and that their particular interests had to be weighed against a wider conception of the public interest. As one councillor put it:

> Voluntary bodies are sometimes a nuisance, but they have a part to play. They can be helpful because they can give you a point of view which you haven't realised. You tend to see things through an official channel after a while and an outside body can give you a fresh insight. Sometimes they're time-wasting, but you shouldn't overlook them.

Fifteen of the twenty-six councillors interviewed could actually recall consulting voluntary organisations in the preceding twelve months. The range of bodies consulted was extremely wide, with no type of organisation being mentioned more than twice. Independent councillors would seem to be generally receptive to advice from local voluntary organisations, but there is no evidence in the case of 'Central' or 'Westward' that any particular organisation exerts any substantial influence.

The councillors: a tentative typology

Newton points out, 'Role orientation studies have a habit of isolating different strands of the representational role and then trying to make some sense of these different strands separately from the others.' [29] However, as Newton emphasises, 'The way in which an elected representative interprets different facets of his job will depend on how he perceives, evaluates and structures his total social and political world'. Newton goes on to construct five role types for councillors based on his Birmingham data.

When the study was being designed, it was felt that it would be difficult to use

Newton's typology in a rural area. It was anticipated that a large proportion of the respondents would fall into the category designated by Newton 'the parochials':

> The political world of the parochial consists primarily of his own ward and of the individuals who bring problems to him . . . their main characteristics are a non-ideological approach to politics together with an implicit belief that politics must be treated on a piecemeal, individual basis. [31]

It was also anticpated that some 'peoples' agents' might be encountered:

> Council members who, like the parochials, are more concerned with individual problems . . . they have a tendency to view their role not simply as that of an unpaid social worker but as a rather special person who, by virtue of popular election and his own individual qualities, serves the function of protecting the population against governmental injustice. [32]

Newton then goes on to distinguish between three types of policy orientation which may be held by councillors: policy advocates who 'discuss their council work within the context of a more or less explicit set of political beliefs and values' [33] policy brokers 'who perform the classical political brokerage role of mediator and reconciler of different interests'; [34] and the policy spokesmen who express a preference 'for being involved in general policy matters' [35] It was not considered that there would be many policy advocates or policy brokers serving on independent councils, although there might be some policy spokesmen. It was anticipated that Newton's typology would have to be modified in the light of the empirical findings of the survey and this proved to be the case.

The typology outlined below contains six categories (although one of these contains only one councillor and might be dispensed with). Assignments to the categories were made on the basis of a councillor's replies to the questionnaire as a whole, although particular attention was paid to the questions relating to trustee-politico-delegate roles, district-ward roles, policy-individual orientations, and a question, 'How would you describe your job of being a council member — what are the most important aspects of that job?'

Ten of the twenty-six respondents were classified as 'parochials': these were sub-divided into two groups, *parochials by inclination* and *parochials by necessity*. The *parochial by inclination* sees his ward as his first priority; he gains most satisfaction from dealing with individual problems and he may actually dislike the whole notion of policy-making. One 'parochial by inclination' described his role on the council in the following terms:

> I think broad policy is far removed from the man in the street, you do far more good by getting a waste pipe fixed in a sink or a street light repaired or a pot hole filled in a road than you can by making broad policy decisions which are tainted by politics. I prefer to get out in the village, pick up problems and do something about it. For example, if the county makes a decision about education, by the time it filters down, a lot of what you put in

is lost, a little practical help is better than theory, people are looking for direct help . . . a good deal of policy is a little out of the reach of the average councillor, it's a professional and specialist job, you need to rely on the officers. In the parish you have the edge.

'Parochials' did differ in the extent to which they went out actively looking for problems and grievances. For example, one commented, 'I am a member of all the churches and chapels in the area, if you do that you have an opportunity of meeting the electorate. I go to (village) on Sunday to meet the men on the cliff, if they have any troubles, they let me know.' On the other hand, another councillor remarked, 'This is a very easy district. I'm very well known, but I don't get a lot of letters. Of the villages I look after, only two have council houses. It's more that the people trust me to look after their affairs and don't bother me too much'.

Of course, too great a concentration on the needs of one's own locality can be self-defeating. As one 'parochial' respondent observed, 'You have to compromise. If you become too parochial you lose the respect and support of other councillors, sometimes you might not put forward your view as strongly as you would wish because you would alienate councillors who would support you on something far more important to your parish. You have to represent the parish within a district framework. Sometimes you need district resources to promote local projects.'

Unlike Birmingham, the 'parochials' are not relatively new councillors; their mean length of service is approximately the same as that for all respondents. Only four have been committee chairmen, but this may simply reflect their preferences. They represent both small towns and villages. Whether a person is a 'parochial' or not would seem to depend very much on his or her personal inclination

Parochials by necessity are newly elected councillors for whom the 'parochial' role is the only one available or the easiest one to fulfill, but who hope to become policy-makers in the long run:

Because I'm new and haven't got much experience, I'm not taking part in policy-making, hopefully that comes eventually. I'm new and I have found looking after individuals rewarding but just recently I've also been involved in seeing policy-making decisions made and later on I shall try to develop that aspect.

Although only two councillors were 'parochials by necessity' compared with eight who were 'parochials by inclination', the 'parochials by necessity' are important in as far as they represent a potential source of future committee chairmen.

Policy-makers were also subdivided into two groups, *policy makers by necessity* and *policy makers by inclination.* Seven councillors were in the latter group. They had the greatest mean length of service of any of the categories (12.7 years). Although they do not neglect the individual problems of their constituents, their preference is for taking broad policy decisions relating to the district as a whole which they see as the real job of the councillor:

Making broad policy is the function of the councillor. The day-to-day

27

problems are to be resolved by our officers. If I have individual problems in my ward, I would see that they were dealt with by the officers. That is not my job.

Something that ought to be pushed is that councillors should be thinking about the whole district and not so much about their own patch. Policy as a whole is more important in the long term than dealing with day-to-day complaints.

Four councillors were classified as *policy-maker by necessity*. These are councillors who prefer a parochial role, but feel that it is no longer viable because of the larger area they have to deal with after reorganisation; or because of their jobs as committee chairmen feel that they have to give priority to district needs and policy-making — but may well revert to a parochial role when they are no longer chairmen. They may be uncertain (usually without justification) about their own ability to cope with a policy-making role:

The making of a policy decision is somewhat harder than helping the individual, helping the individual is a little more gratifying if you get success, some policy decisions I sometimes wonder whether I'm big enough even to contemplate them, although it's my job to do it.

Dovetailers are councillors who see the potential tension between their ward/individual and policy/district roles, but are consciously trying to integrate the two. The term is derived from one councillor's response, 'I'm doing a dovetailing trick'. These are councillors who recognise the importance of looking after one's ward in a rural area, but who also see the necessity of taking a broader perspective. Of course, in one sense all councillors are 'dovetailers'. No councillor is so obsessed with policy making that he will neglect an individual constituent with a grievance; no councillor is so parochial that he will not vote on a general matter affecting the district as a whole. The four 'dovetailers' are councillors with a strong commitment to their particular ward, who nevertheless are also making a special effort to contribute to the development of the district as an entity:

Being a rural representative . . . people must know you personally, they must trust you as someone with whom they can discuss their personal and private matters . . . one is a confidant, a confessor and a comforter — the churches, the ministers have become less and less, you are particularly required to see electors not only regarding council affairs, but on a multitude of family questions: legal and financial difficulties, marriage problems, childrens problems and old age problems. You cannot help getting involved in details, but you've got to be man enough to help determine future policy.

'Dovetailers' often display a special concern with the integration of the district:

One must recognise the great difficulty at the moment because of this recent local government reorganisation, particularly in an area like this where the geographical and historical background is of separate and independent communities . . . We should at least try to make the new system work by consent within the district as a whole. Inevitably we are all in some ways parochial — we can't help it — but we have to try and create the conditions in which intransigence would slowly pass away.

Finally, it was not possible to classify one councillor other than as a 'peoples' agent', but it may be that future studies would find that this categorisation was not necessary in the study of other district councils. This would then give a typology of three basic roles, with two of the roles being subdivided into two further categories giving an overall fivefold typology.

The typology constructed here is open to objection in so far as it involves some interpretation of people's motivations on the basis of interview material. However, it is clear that Newton's typology, which may aid the understanding of the roles of urban councillors, is not applicable in a rural context. It should be added that it is not implied that one 'type' of councillor is to be preferred to another. District councils need councillors who have a good knowledge of particular localities and who follow up individual grievances and councillors who are prepared to look at the long-term needs of the district as a whole. Both 'Westward' and 'Central' benefitted from having a mixture of both kinds of councillor.

It is argued that the typology developed in this chapter goes some way towards helping us to understand the patterns of decision-making on an independent council. Many councillors are clearly preoccupied with the impact of policy on their locality: they will carefully scrutinise planning proposals affecting their areas; ensure that enough council houses are provided to keep village families together; press for better recreational facilities for their ward. They keep in close touch with parish councils in their wards and, as far as possible, with individual electors, thus ensuring that grievances and shortcomings in council services such as refuse disposal are rapidly brought to the attention of the local authority. However, all councillors act collectively, whatever their personal role orientations, to take decisions which affect the district as a whole. The typology helps us to understand the individual behaviour of councillors. It may help us to understand particular collective decisions: for example, if a matter affecting a particular ward is being discussed, 'parochials' may defer to the view of the councillor from that ward, whereas 'policy makers' may give priority to the application of district policy. Nevertheless, the typology does not tell us all that we need to know about how an independent council behaves as a council.

Ministerialism

How, then, does a council made up of independents make decisions? Dyer has argued that 'Independent politics is essentially administration without strategy, and "policy" can be defined as the approach taken to each item as it presents itself'. [36] In the case of Kincardineshire, Dyer found that 'The most important aspect of local government in Kincardineshire was not so much the absence of class conflict, but the almost complete absence of any conflict at all'. [37] The absence of conflict — or at least conflict about substantive issues — may well characterise politics in small face-to-face communities. However, district councils serving a number of communities have to make resource allocation decisions which necessarily raise the questions of principle which form the basis of party political debate.

One possible pattern of decision-making on an independent council is that a considerable influence will be exerted by the committee chairmen working with the relevant chief officers. In Cheshire, Lee found that 'The leading members of the council and the chief officers formed a kind of ministerialist party.' [38] Thus 'an understanding of county government requires the application of a well-worn distinction of British constitutional history, the division between "court" and "country", between "ministerialists" and "anti-ministerialists".' [39] It is suggested that the notion of ministerialism may usefully be applied to the examination of the decision-making processes on district councils controlled by independents. It should be emphasised that the notion of 'ministerialism' does not mean that the committee chairmen and chief officers conspire against the rest of the council (although it may be seen in this light), but rather that they formulate policy for submission to the committees and the council in the light of their knowledge of the preferences of council members.

It has already been pointed out that unpredictability is a feature of the electoral process in nonpartisan areas, because election outcomes can be determined by a large number of random factors, instead of largely by the relative standing of the major parties nationally at the time of the election. Without an assertion of 'ministerialism' this unpredictability can extend to the decision making processes of the local authority. Consider the contrast between a council made up of independents and one dominated by a single party which makes use of the caucus system and requires its councillors to adhere to the party 'whip'. In its 'purest' form, this system should operate as follows: policies are discussed and agreed in the caucus and then implemented through the use of the group's voting majority on the council and its committees. Of course, in practice all kinds of difficulties can arise with such a system. Nevertheless, the officers can be reasonably assured that once a policy has been adopted by the majority party, it will be adopted by the whole council.

There is a reasonable degree of predictability in a party-dominated system; an independent council, on the other hand, tends towards unpredictability. There is no assurance that a policy adopted by a committee will be adopted by the whole council; for example, a decision by the housing committee to sell or not to sell council houses may well be overturned by the whole council. It will be difficult to predict in advance what the decision will be. In the independent council, the meeting of the full council is far more important than in a council dominated by a single party. Spencer notes in his study of Labour-dominated 'Aberton' that 'as party politics increasingly influenced the scene, the council meetings ceased to be decision-making occasions in the normal sense of the word'. [40] They were mainly an occasion which would 'tarnish or enhance the image of either party in the eyes of the press, and ultimately of the wider public'. [41] On an independent council, it will often be the vote of the council meeting that decides major policies; they are decision-making occasions in the real sense of the word.

The importance of the full council meeting will vary from one independent council to another; in some councils, a 'ministerialist' system will be established relatively easily and committee chairmen and chief officers, working as a team, will play a substantial role in the decision-making process. However, there is always likely to be some resistance to 'ministerialism' among independent councillors, although the intensity of this resistance will vary from place to place and time to time. The doctrines of 'independent politics' rest on a belief that the best decisions are made by the individual considering each decision 'on its merits' in the light of 'the facts', his conscience and his knowledge of the district he represents. Councillors are likely to be suspicious of any attempt to undermine the status and powers of the full council and to upgrade the importance of its committees.

The general impression gained from the interviews and observation at council meetings was that 'Central' approximated in some respects to a 'ministerialist' pattern of decision-making, but that there was a great deal of resistance on 'Westward' to the development of any decision-making pattern of a 'ministerialist' kind. Not only does 'Westward' have more scheduled council meetings in a year than 'Central' (eight compared with six), special and extraordinary meetings of the full council play a significant role in the decision-making process (for example, there were seven in the period from May 1976 to January 1977).

Despite the apparent significance of the full council, members of 'Westward' display some anxiety about incipient 'ministerialist' tendencies in the decision-making process. This anxiety led in 1976 to an extraordinary meeting of the council, called by more than half its members, to discuss the Council's standing orders. The sponsors of the motion stated: 'It seems obvious that there is much dissension amongst council members because of the number of minutes on the full Council agenda that seemingly have been resolved by any of the four major committees. If this procedure continues it is a negation of what we are sent by the electorate to do as we cannot discuss matters affecting that same electorate. The real debating forum should be the main council rather than the full committee stage to give full discussion on contentious minutes.' This argument was developed further at the extraordinary meeting when it was stated that in committee something might be won by just one vote so that the council could be run by a quarter of its members. Members were faced with a motion which sought to suspend the delegated powers of all committees except the Development Services Committee; this motion was defeated, but the council did agree to re-examine its standing orders. Subsequently, an attempt has been made to increase the proportion of recommendations to resolutions sent from committees to the full council.

In fact, the proportion of councillors on any one committee is larger on 'Westward' than on 'Central' (over half as against just over one-third). In addition whereas 'Central' has the usual post-reorganisation Policy & Resources Committee with a series of functional sub-committees, 'Westward' has a different arrangement.

31

In 1976 the 'Westward' council abolished its Policy & Resources Committee and replaced it by a Resource Committee which does not have a structure of sub-committees under it. Apparently, it was felt that under the initial post-reorganisation system members often went over the same problem three times (in sub-committee, Policy & Resources and on the full council). A further reason was the strong aversion of many councillors to the notion of 'policy' which was dropped from the committee's title. As one councillor put it, 'This council detests the name 'policy'.'

Councillors in both authorities were asked 'How important do you think the meeting of the full council is in the work of the District Council?' and 'Do you think that the division of responsibility between the council meeting and the committees is about right or would you like to see it altered in any way?' The answers to these questions revealed a greater difference between the two sets of respondents than on any other matter.

In 'Central', all thirteen respondents thought that the division of responsibility between the council meeting and the committees was, in general, about right. Respondents differed about the part played by the council meeting in the decision-making process: in general, six said that they thought it was very important and seven thought that it was not very important. This distinction is in some ways arbitrary; most members seemed to agree that the committees were more important, but that it was sometimes possible for a member to overturn a decision in full council and this was an important 'safety valve'. Perhaps the best way of reflecting respondents' opinions is to give a selection of replies:

> It's important because you've got to have it in a negative way. You must have a means whereby one committee making a recommendation can be shot down by the council as a whole.
>
> The council meeting is the last resort to challenge everything and if you put a good case you can turn the tide. (I think that the division of responsibility between the council meeting and the committees) is about right. Some people feel that committees have too much power because of their delegated authority, but the Policy & Resources Committee is a safety valve. If you made fewer decisions in committee, you'd get very long council meetings which wouldn't achieve a great deal. It depends what you want to do as a member.
>
> The committee structure which we've got at (Central) gives ample opportunity for anything to be thoroughly aired and debated before the full council meeting.

All the 'Westward' respondents agreed that the council meeting was important; the division of opinion was between those who thought that the council meeting was not as important as it ought to be and that too many decisions were taken by the committees (five) and those who thought that the balance of responsibility between the two was about right (eight). It was clear that some of the councillors held very strong views about the issue of the role of the council meeting in the decision-making process:

> Very controversial. The old (name of) council made all decisions, now committees are making resolutions . . .

> We run a Resource Committee and a lot goes to that which is cutting a lot of interest out of the full council. The main standing committees have the power to make resolutions and this can only mean that the main council is not the ultimate authority . . . a view very strongly held by many people is that the ultimate authority must always be the full council. It's the only way in which most councillors feel they are in control.

Other councillors stressed the role of committees and committee chairmen in the decision-making process:

> I would like to think that the committees are responsible for their duties, the members of the council should put their faith in the deliberations of the committees, on occasions this isn't done.

> Given that you had people in local government for a period of years, I would like to think that when they elected chairmen and vice-chairmen of the committees, they would have confidence in those chairmen, you would have a number of people whose opinions the chairman of the council would be able to take as representing the committees.

In addition to having differing views about the roles of the council meeting and the committees in the decision-making process, some 'ministerialists' and 'anti-ministerialists' also differed in terms of their attitude towards officers and their views about policy-making. For example, one 'anti-ministerialist' argued, 'Once you become a committee chairman you are an officers' stooge. You've got to do what they tell you to do.' Another 'anti-ministerialist' commented, 'The Resource Committee is tied up with the officer management set-up and this is where ordinary councillors feel they are not being permitted to discharge their primary function, this is where they feel they are being directed by officers and not achieving what they desire by frank and open debate'. By way of contrast, a 'ministerialist' argued, 'I don't think there ought to be a dividing line at all between officers and councillors, there ought to be mutual respect one for the other so that it becomes an exchange of views rather than 'us and them'.' As one might expect, none of the 'anti-ministerialists' were 'policy-makers by inclination'. As one of them stressed, 'I am not a great believer in policy . . . I don't believe in making policy too far ahead, each individual case should be decided on its merits'. One respondent summarised the situation on 'Westward' in the following terms, 'There is always a tremendous suspicion that something is going on, that 'they' are up to something, therefore the council is the forum in which the battles are fought'. It should be added that some councillors expressed the view that the decision-making processes of the council had been working more satisfactorily since the adjustments following the extraordinary council meeting referred to earlier.

How can the differences between the decision-making processes in 'Central' and

'Westward' be accounted for? It may be argued that the need for consistency in policy will tend to generate pressures for a 'ministerialist' pattern of decision-making on councils controlled by independents, but these pressures will be counteracted by the suspicion of ministerialism which stems from the values held by the proponents of 'independent politics'. These values are particularly likely to be asserted by new and imperfectly socialised members of the council; thus one of the factors affecting the propensity towards a 'ministerialist' pattern of decision-making on independent councils may be the turnover rate of councillors. Some of the 'Westward' councillors drew attention to the large influx of new members on to their council in 1976; however, although a third of the members returned were new, this proportion was the same as on 'Central'. A further factor which councillors drew attention to was the differences between 'Westward' and the predecessor authorities in terms of the strength of the norms relating to the behaviour of new members. As one councillor recalled, 'When I was first a councillor, it was accepted that one didn't speak for the first three years or so, an alderman said to me: 'You just watch points and if you want to know anything ask me.' Now new councillors start making points at their first meeting.' Undoubtedly, informal social controls are weaker on the new, larger councils and there may well be less deference towards seniority. Moreover, there is probably more risk of a senior member suffering an electoral defeat (a risk enhanced by the abolition of the aldermanic system in the boroughs). The unpredictable outcomes of nonpartisan elections may damage a developing 'ministerialist' system of decision making. All these factors help us to understand the obstacles in the way of a 'ministerialist' pattern of decision-making, but they do not explain the differences between 'Central' and 'Westward'.

One possibility is that geographical rivalries between predecessor authorities may be more intense on 'Westward' than on 'Central'. There was some evidence of rivalry between the two main towns in 'Westward', both resorts formerly organised as non-county boroughs. However, there was no particular geographical pattern to the distribution of 'ministerialists' and 'anti-ministerialists'. Moreover, there was some feeling in 'Central' among rural members that too much time was spent on the affairs of the former non-county borough, whereas one of its representatives expressed the view that insufficient recognition was given to its status as an 'international little town'.

It would seem that two factors account for the differences between the two authorities studied here. First, 'Westward' is a genuine independent council, whereas 'Central' is nominally controlled by the Conservatives. In fact, although the Conservative group does not play a very great part in the decision-making process on 'Central', it does provide an additional, informal mechanism for resolving disputes before they reach the council chamber. Indeed, it was suggested by one independent that a potentially contentious issue had been dealt with in this way.

Second, 'Westward' has a far more 'turbulent' environment than 'Central' which produces far more pressing problems for resolution. 'Central', of course, had its problems, particularly that of reducing the length of its housing list in times of financial stringency. However, 'Westward' appeared to have a wider range of problems, some intractable. As outlined by councillors, the major problems faced by 'Westward' were: 'We have to operate within an area of very low income with a great many old and dilapidated properties' (housing problems were exacerbated by the number of 'second homes'); 'the problem of employment, although as a council we can do very little about that because of our geographical position'; 'the effect on the environment of the tourist trade' ('Central' has a tourist trade, but it doesn't have a long coastline). In addition, the most important immediate problem has been the transformation of a traditional local industry in a way that has benefitted some local people and harmed others; two of the special council meetings referred to earlier have been to deal with problems arising from this question. One also has to take into account the greater political heterogeneity of 'Westward'.

It is suggested that the following factors may have some bearing on whether or not an independent council develops a system of decision-making that may be described as 'ministerialist':

1. A high turnover rate of councillors will make it more difficult to develop a 'ministerialist' system of decision-making. However, the turnover rate itself is a crude indicator. One also has to take account of the effectiveness of arrangements for socialising new members into the procedural norms of the council; such norms are likely to become better established and more widely accepted by councillors as rivalries between predecessor authorities recede into the background and the district becomes accepted as the major framework of reference. A further consideration is the predictability or otherwise of local elections; how 'safe' are the seats of key members of the council?

2. The answer to this last question will depend, in part, on the heterogeneity of the local political environment (is it Conservative-dominant or are there Conservative-Liberal or Conservative-Nationalist tensions?) and on how 'turbulent' and problem-laden the local environment is. The seats of sitting councillors are more likely to be at risk in localities where there are serious political rivalries and a number of contentious local issues. Even more important, these environmental pressures can affect the decision-making processes of the council itself by creating more points of potential tension and conflict.

3. Attention must also be paid to the role of any party political representatives on the council. For example, a small Labour group on an otherwise independent council may encourage other councillors who are anti-Socialist in sympathy to try to co-ordinate the work of a council. Once a group holds a preponderance of the seats on a council, it is in a position to exert a considerable informal influence on the decision-making process even if it does not 'whip' its members. In other words, the tendency towards a 'ministerialist' system of decision-making increases as the proportion of party political councillors increases.

One further question remains: what are the 'policy consequences of non-partisanship'? [43] In his study of nonpartisanship in the United States (admittedly a somewhat different phenomenon), Hawley argues that nonpartisan city elections 'foster public policies that are relatively conservative and unresponsive to demands for social change and for the aggressive use of governmental power to remedy social problems'. [43] It is often argued in Britain that independents are either concealed Conservatives or more conservative than the Conservatives.

This latter view is clearly an oversimplified one. Apart from any other considerations, independent councils are subject to (increasing) government intervention in the same way as any other council and this acts as a constraint on their ability to develop distinctive policies should they wish to do so. Nevertheless, the sources of influence on local government expenditure decisions are complex and diverse and local councils do have some measure of latitude in such key areas as housing policy.

The most serious conflicts on 'Westward' council have been over the general level of council expenditure, particularly on staffing, and on housing. On the whole, the advocates of further expenditure cuts over and above those already agreed by the council have been defeated, although the votes are sometimes close and they have won occasional victories.

Attacks on council house building programmes have also been fought off. The sale of council houses is, of course, potentially one of the most contentious issues. This issue offers an interesting illustration of the way in which independent councils do not necessarily automatically follow Conservative policies. The 'Westward' council initially decided not to sell council houses, although it is reviewing the issue at the time of writing.

One of the most contentious issues on 'Westward' since its formation has been the proposed development as a council estate of a site of some fifty acres on the outskirts of the largest town. Many members of the public objected to this proposal on the grounds that it would spoil an attractive piece of countryside. Local concern about the effect on the environment was not the only consideration influencing the council; the matter was considered against the background of what the council termed 'the deteriorating economic situation and a further cutback in the housing programme announced by the Chancellor in his mini-Budget'. This linkage between national decisions and local decisions is well known and understood in Britain; the government's current policy preferences are transmitted to local authorities and absorbed into their decision-making processes through well-established channels. What was unusual about this particular case was the intervention of the local Member of Parliament; as Ashford observes, 'the national-local political link is virtually denied to be operative in Britain'. [44] In a speech in the constituency on the Saturday before the Council made its decision, the local Member of Parliament argued that it would be wrong to proceed with large-scale housing developments in the prevailing climate. This statement was clearly taken as a reference to the 'Westward' scheme and the Chairman of the Council expressed regret that the Member of Parliament had not approached him before making his statement 'to learn the full facts'. At its meeting, the council decided by nineteen votes to twelve to withdraw its compulsory purchase orders for the land. However, at a later meeting, the council agreed in principle by nineteen votes to twelve to acquire the land for development. It was argued by the supporters of acquisition that the council had a duty as a housing authority to build houses, that there was a proven need for more houses and that the site was the only suitable one for a large-scale development.

Local Conservatives also suffered a rebuff over another issue. When the Council issued new planning regulations for conservation areas, these were condemned by the constituency Conservative Association as 'an excess of interference with the freedom of the individual to maintain his property'. The Association wrote a letter of protest to the council and also informed the local Member of Parliament of their displeasure with the council. At a subsequent meeting of the 'Westward' planning committee, attempts to rescind the regulations and to call for the resignation of the chief planning officer were defeated. Neither of these incidents suggests that it is easy for either constituency Conservative Associations or Conservative Members of Parliament to influence the actions of independent councils.

Independent councillors are not 'merely undeclared Conservatives'. [45] They may often be (although they can be Liberal, Nationalist or Labour in national politics) but their behaviour on a council may differ from that of official Conservative representatives. The independent politics of district councils in rural areas is often more complex than it at first appears to be. In general, independent councils display a tendency towards greater unpredictability than party-controlled councils in terms of both their electoral and decision-making processes. The character of these processes, and the policy outcomes which emerge from them, may vary a great deal in accordance with local circumstances.

Notes

[1] T. Hjellum, 'The Politicisation of Local Government: Rates of Change, Conditioning Factors, Effects on Political Culture', *Scandinavian Political Studies,* vol.2, 1966, pp.69–93.

[2] Norfolk, 4; Suffolk, 4; Hampshire, 3; Oxfordshire, 3; Northamptonshire, 3; Essex, 3; Cambridge, 2; Wiltshire, 2; East Sussex, 2; Derbyshire, 2; Nottinghamshire, 2; Lincolnshire, 2; Kent, 1; Hertfordshire, 1; Buckinghamshire, 1; West Sussex, 1; Leicestershire, 1; Warwickshire, 1.

[3] See Chapter Four for data on this point.

[4] J. Gyford, *Local Politics in Britain,* Croom Helm, London 1976, p.62.

[5] Ratepayers gained three seats from Independents; the Liberals gained one seat from the Conservatives and one Independent changed her label to Liberal.

[6] J.M. Lee, B. Wood, B.W. Solomon, P. Walters, *The Scope of Local Initiative,* Martin Robinson, London 1974, p.115.

[7] Ibid., p.188.

[8] Ibid., p.190.

[9] Ibid., p.114.

[10] Ibid., p.114.

[11] See Chapter Four.

[12] In 'Central' councillors were listed alphabetically by party group, excluding chairmen, and every n^{th} councillor was selected to make up the required number; in 'Westward' councillors excluding chairmen were listed alphabetically and every n^{th} councillor was selected to provide the required number. Two 'Central' councillors refused to be interviewed, and one in 'Westward' could not be contacted, giving an overall response rate of ninety per cent.

[13] 'Central' District coincided with the boundaries of one constituency; most of 'Westward' formed a constituency, but part of the district was in another constituency, also Conservative held. The Liberal candidate came second in both main constituencies in October 1974.

[14] Two prominent landowning families in the area are not represented on the council, although four of their number are magistrates.

[15] M. Dyer, *Independent Politics in Kincardineshire,* University of Aberdeen Ph.D. thesis, 1973, p.497.

[16] Ibid., p.527.

[17] I am indebted to Jeffrey Stanyer for drawing my attention to the notion of a 'political occupation'.

[18] K. Newton, *Second City Politics,* Oxford University Press, London 1976, p.16.

[19] K. Spencer, 'Party Politics and the Processes of Local Democracy in an English Town Council' in A. Richards and A. Kuper (eds.), *Councils in Action,* Cambridge University Press, London 1971, pp.171–201.

[20] Ibid., p.180.

[21] Ibid., p.182.

[22] Ibid., p.182.

[23] No questions were asked about political affiliation, although some respondents volunteered this information. The judgement is therefore an impressionistic one.

[24] A.J. Beith, 'An Anti-Labour Caucus: the Case of the Northumberland Voters' Association', *Policy and Politics,* vol.2, no.2, 1974, pp.153–65, p.155.

[25] The pioneer work in this field is J.C. Wahlke, H. Eulau, W. Buchanan, Le Roy C. Ferguson, *Explorations in Legislative Behaviour,* Wiley, New York 1962. For a useful review of the applicability of role analysis to the study of British local councillors see J. Gyford, op. cit., chapter two.

[26] Newton, op. cit., p.118.

[27] Ibid., p.128.

[28] Ibid., p.86.

[29] Ibid., p.136.

[30] Ibid., p.136.

[31] Ibid., pp.137–8.

[32] Ibid., p.138.

[33] Ibid., p.140.

[34] Ibid., p.141.

[35] Ibid., p.142.

[36] Dyer, op. cit., p.795.

[37] Ibid., p.271.

[38] J.M. Lee, *Social Leaders and Public Persons: a Study of County Government in Cheshire since 1888,* Clarendon Press, Oxford 1963, p.190.

[39] Ibid., p.191.

[40] Spencer, op. cit., p.189.

[41] Ibid., p.189.

[42] W.D. Hawley, *Nonpartisan Elections and the Case for Party Politics,* Wiley, New York 1973, p.5.

[43] Ibid., p.5.

[44] D.E. Ashford, *Democracy, Decentralisation and Decisions in Subnational Politics,* Sage Publications, Beverly Hills 1976, p.34.

[45] Gyford, op. cit., p.96, reviewing other commentators.

2　The politics of the unusual

In this chapter an analytical framework is presented which attempts to explain the variations in the activity rates and level of electoral success of ratepayers and residents movements in different local political systems in England and Wales before local government reorganisation. [1] As Stanyer has pointed out, the occurrence of these 'purely local parties' is 'hard to explain'. [2] Nevertheless, it is argued that their incidence is not random, but that it can be related to special features of certain types of local political system. It is not argued that 'purely local parties' arose only in the circumstances elaborated in this chapter or that they necessarily developed when a particular combination of socio-political circumstances was present in a local political system. It is, however, argued that they are more likely to occur and be successful in some types of local political system than in others.

The analytical framework developed and tested in this chapter was evolved before local government reorganisation. Some of the local political systems in which 'purely local parties' were most likely to occur (e.g., small resort towns forming an urban district) have disappeared as a result of reorganisation. However, in order to understand patterns of local politics, one must not only examine their present mode of operation but also how they have developed in the past. Moreover, it is argued that the analytical framework does have some continuing relevance, although it needs to be modified to take account of the effects of local government reorganisation and a number of other developments. A modified analytical framework is presented in Chapter Four.

'Purely local political parties' have been defined by Stanyer as 'parties which do not contest national elections and which are formed for political purposes in the locality only, though they may later join a loose federation of similar groups'. [3] Most of these parties use labels such as 'ratepayer' or 'resident', although 'tenants' parties have emerged in one or two localities. Purely local parties may be divided into two broad types. A distinction may be made between the 'concealed Conservative' type of local party and the 'genuine' local party which is prepared to fight an electoral contest against a Conservative candidate. In making a similar distinction, Steed points out that 'A Ratepayer group opposed by Conservatives may still be largely Conservative in make-up, or one not opposed by the Conservatives may be quite innocent of collusion with the Conservative party'. [4]

The definition does, in fact, give rise to a number of conceptual and practical problems. An interesting refinement to the original definition has been suggested by Beith who argues that the 'Anti-Labour caucus' is 'an interesting variant of the "concealed Conservative group" ' and 'needs to be placed in a distinct category'. [5] Beith sees caucus parties as organisations of 'councillors and aldermen on a single local authority with no external organisation'. [6]

Caucus parties like the Northumberland Voters' Association discussed by Beith would seem to be relatively rare. The more usual 'concealed Conservative' party does have some form of external organisation, even if it is relatively rudimentary. The central difficulty with the distinction between 'concealed' and 'genuine' parties is that 'concealed Conservative' parties (Progressives, Moderates, Citizens etc.) may be the only organised opposition to the Labour Party in a particular locality over a period of time, but this situation may change when the local Conservative Party decides that it would rather be represented by Conservatives by label than by conservatives by inclination. In these circumstances, the 'concealed Conservatives' may not simply stand aside or allow themselves to be recruited as official Conservative candidates; their opposition to party politics in local government may lead them into a head-on electoral clash with the Conservative nominees. For example, in the 1968 municipal elections in Edinburgh, 'direct clashes of Tories and Progressives occurred . . . Conservatives standing regardless of the effect that splitting the right wing support might have'. [7] In such circumstances, the 'concealed' Conservative party becomes a 'genuine' local party in terms of the definition.

The definitional problems are, then, considerable, but there is a distinction between parties like the Bristol 'Citizens' whose links with the Conservatives were 'so close . . . and so similar to those in other cities between Conservative council groups and the Conservative party that it would be misleading to attach significance to the difference in nomenclature' [8] and movements like the Residents' Associations in Billericay discussed in the next chapter who offered a direct electoral challenge to the Conservatives. The existence of ambiguous cases should not be allowed to obscure the significance of the fundamental distinction.

For the reasons explained in the introduction, this study concentrates on the 'genuine' local parties. In what socio-economic and political circumstances are 'genuine' local parties likely to arise and be successful? There has been remarkably little systematic research on this subject, [9] and the analytical framework reported in this study was developed in an attempt to categorise the different situations in British local politics in which such parties were likely to emerge.

The fundamental premise on which the analytical framework is based is that 'genuine' local parties are the product of conflicts inherent in particular local political situations which are not easily articulated in terms of the 'left-right' division of the national political parties. Or in other words, such local parties are most likely to arise where local circumstances divide people who may share similar views on national affairs.

An important distinction may be made between the *trigger action* that provokes the initial formation of a local party, and the *underlying sustaining factors* that create the conditions for its survival. Any council may take an unpopular decision which could provide the *trigger action* for the formation of a local party. However, unless the decision is of a very special type (which will be discussed later), it is predicted that the resultant indignation among the electorate will not lead to the formation of a local party unless *underlying sustaining factors* exist in the local political system. Or in other words, if a local party born in a sudden outburst of indignation is to maintain its momentum, there must be a serious conflict in the community which divides the citizens on other than national party lines. [10]

A typology of underlying sustaining factors will be discussed shortly. Meanwhile, it should be stressed that it is the underlying sustaining factors rather than the trigger actions which are theoretically important. The trigger action may occur at any time and place, but underlying sustaining factors will be limited to a relatively small proportion of communities, and it is in those communities that purely local parties are likely to be successful.

For example, on a Bristol estate studied by Bracey, a proposal to build a public house on a central site triggered off the formation of a Residents' Association which subsequently secured several seats on the local council. [11] However, it may be argued that it was the existence of what is subsequently described as an 'expanding area' situation, and not the initial grievance, that explains the success of a local party in this case. As Bracey points out, the initial campaign over the public house was followed by other campaigns on problems common to expanding areas — inadequate educational facilities and the lack of a playing field, health centre and other amenities.

Eight situations in which 'genuine local parties' are particularly likely to arise are distinguished. Two of these are of major importance (the 'rapidly expanding area' in which a great deal of new housing development is taking place and the resort town). Six are of lesser importance — towns where a major decision has to be taken involving the question, 'What sort of town shall ours be?'; on council estates where events activate tenant solidarity; where middle class radicals are offended by local authority decisions or attitudes; where there is a sharp increase in the rates burden borne by the householder or particular groups of householders (other than in situations discussed above); in areas with large populations drawn from minority ethnic groups; and in areas where there has been a serious split in one of the national political parties. Each of these cases will be considered in turn, in order to show how they are social bases for conflict which differ from the customary issues which divide the national parties.

Aggregate data analysis has acquired a new popularity in the study of electoral behaviour at the national level in recent years; in particular, considerable use has been made of census data to explore relationships between the social composition of constituencies and their patterns of voting behaviour. However, aggregate data can also make a substantial contribution to the study of local politics.

Two sets of aggregate electoral data were used to test the analytical framework developed in this chapter. One set took local authorities other than county councils and rural districts in England and Wales as the unit of analysis; data was collected on the success of 'genuine local parties' in these authorities between 1955-58 and 1960-68 and related to a range of indicators derived from census data. However, taking the local authority as the unit of analysis poses a number of problems; not least that the variation on any given social indicator within an authority may often be greater than the variation between authorities. For example, two local authorities may have a similar proportion of their populations designated as non-manual on the basis of census material, but one may contain equally balanced upper middle class and working districts, whereas the other may contain fewer upper middle class persons, but a large number of junior nonmanual workers. Nevertheless, this data does have some value in so far as it permits the investigation of broad national trends (aggregate analysts have not hesitated to use constituencies as units of analysis). However, to supplement this national data analysis, a set of data was also collected for Devon for the period 1955-68 (excluding Plymouth and the rural districts) using the ward as the unit of analysis. [12] The correlations obtained from the Devon data were in the same direction as the correlations obtained from the national data, but were generally stronger, which is what one would expect given the more precise nature of the Devon data.

The results of the aggregate analyses will be presented here in summary form. The reader who is interested in a more detailed presentation or who wishes to examine the problems encountered in the operationalisation of the variables used is advised to turn to the author's doctoral thesis. [13] In this account, an attempt has been made to draw a balance between being excessively technical and failing to point out how the techniques used could have influenced the results obtained.

Before proceeding to the presentation of the data, it is necessary to make one technical point. The dependent variable in the case of the national data is the percentage of seats held by 'genuine local parties' on each council over the period studied. In the case of the Devon data, two dependent variables were used: the mean percentage share of the vote obtained by 'genuine local parties' in each ward over the period studied and 'genuine local party activity', defined as the number of seats contested by 'genuine local parties' in each ward between 1955 and 1968 expressed as a percentage of the total number of seats available during the period (excluding by-elections but including casual vacancies filled at annual or triennial elections).

'Purely local parties' and the middle class

In the national data analysis, the strongest relationship recorded between an independent variable and the dependent variable of 'genuine local party' strength was the highly significant positive correlation between percentage non-manual and 'genuine local party' strength. Although statistically significant, the relationship found in the national data was still a relatively weak one ($r = .18$, increasing to .23 when councils dominated by independents are excluded from the data set). In the Devon data, the correlations obtained between percentage non-manual and 'genuine local party' strength were higher ($r = .29$; $r = .32$, 'genuine local party' activity). In the case of Devon, correlations with percentage 'professional and managerial' were also calculated but were found to be lower than those for percentage 'non-manual'. [14] ($r = .2$, 'genuine local party' strength; $r = .24$ 'genuine local party' activity). These findings tentatively suggest that, in Devon at any rate, it is not the more prosperous sections of the middle class who are making the greatest

43

contribution to the electoral success and activity of 'genuine local parties'. The more general point that has to be borne in mind is that social class indicators are less useful for predicting 'genuine local party' success than the electoral success in local politics of the major national parties (for example, the product-moment correlation between percentage non-manual and Labour strength was $-.55$). Ratepayer and similar movements do tend to draw support from the non-manual sections of the population and their leadership does tend to be drawn from the middle class (of forty-three activists interviewed during the course of the study, all but four were in the non-manual sections of the populations, 71 per cent of the total being in the Registrar General's Social Classes 2 and 3, non-manual). However, their differential success cannot be explained simply in terms of the geographical distribution of different social classes. Ratepayer movements (particularly before reorganisation) were generally not successful outside middle class areas, but such movements did not develop in the majority of middle class areas.

Population size

One factor which was found to be relevant in explaining the differential success of 'purely local parties' was the population size of the local authority area. It was found that there were relatively few 'genuine local parties' in the local authority areas with small populations. However, as population size increased, the incidence of 'genuine local party' activity also increased, reaching its highest level in the 60,000 – 100,000 population grouping. Evidently, as population size increased, a factor which inhibited 'genuine local party' formation decreased in significance. However, in large communities of over 100,000 population a different inhibiting factor came into operation, exerting a restraining influence on 'genuine local party' activity. In the 60,000 – 100,000 population grouping, the influence of the first factor had decreased to a negligible level and the second factor was not yet sufficiently strong to inhibit the formation and success of 'genuine local parties'. Thus, forty-five per cent of local authorities in the 60,000 – 100,000 population grouping experienced 'genuine local party' activity during the period studied.

What were these two factors? As far as small communities were concerned, the report of the *Community Attitudes Survey* commented: 'It has been striking that in many areas of investigation, especially those dealing with qualitative aspects of community feeling, a quite recognisable variation in response is shown by electors living in the smaller urban authority areas . . . (One difference is that) they possess the largest average number of adult friends, and more frequently discriminate in fact between people in and outside their "home area" on the grounds of the greater friendliness of the former'. [15]

What is the political significance of the existence of these stronger friendship ties in small communities? One consequence before reorganisation was that many of these small authorities maintained nonpartisan political systems; the incidence of nonpartisanship was inversely related to population size. [16] However, even when local authorities dominated by independents were removed from the data set, low population size still exerted an inhibiting effect on 'genuine local party' activity. Two factors would seem to be of importance in explaining this tendency. First, it is a fundamental proposition of community conflict studies that close friendship ties of the sort described minimise the likelihood of open political conflict. Second, in a small community, residents may feel that their local councillors are more accessible and responsive and that there is no need to create alternative structures (such as ratepayers associations) for the articulation of their views. The report of the *Community Attitudes Survey* does indeed remark that 'with increasing size of governmental unit, electors feel a greater need to call upon a representative who might speak for them . . . (the evidence) may also suggest that some degree of alienation − or of inaccessibility − comes into being among local authorities of greater size'. [17]

Population size is not, of course, a factor of overriding importance. Two communities with a similar population size may differ significantly in their social structure. The first may be a socially homogeneous unit; the second may be socially polarised between 'locals' and retired 'newcomers' who may find it necessary to engage in political activity to counteract their isolation from the established community.

If social ties in social communities are too tightly knit to readily permit local party formation, social ties in large communities are often too 'loose'. As David Berry comments, 'There is considerable American evidence to show that as size of community and level of urbanisation of the community increases, then the level of participation in voluntary organisations declines . . . it is (in large urbanised communities) that local community ties are weakest and where, consequently, social relations are more likely to be atomised'. [18]

Whilst this statement would seem to be to some extent applicable to large British cities, it must be qualified by two reservations. First, 'urban villages' may survive in particular areas of large cities. In these areas, there may be intensive kinship and friendship ties and/or extensive participation in voluntary organisations. Moreover, changed circumstances may lead to a renewal of social relationships and an increase in levels of participation. A perceived shared threat (as, for example, that posed by a redevelopment plan) may promote a revival of communal ties. 'Community action' and 'community development' teams have been active in many 'inner city' areas in recent years, although it should be pointed out that the ideologies of many of the members of these teams leads them to favour more radical forms of political action than electoral activity.

Not only do large cities generally offer an unfavourable social environment for the formation of new local political movements, but even those movements which do form may be deterred from contesting local elections by certain aspects of the political power structure of large cities. In a medium-sized urban district with, say, a total of sixteen council seats divided among four wards (a not uncommon pattern before reorganisation) it was not an unrealistic expectation for a 'genuine local party' to consider that it could organise sufficiently well in enough of the wards to make a bid for control of the council. However, it is much more difficult to construct a city-wide organisation to contest, say, twenty wards in order to gain control of a council with sixty seats for councillors. A ratepayer or similar movement may consider that it has a better chance of influencing local decisions if it remains as a pure interest group and does not contest elections. As one residents' association activist who was interviewed in the course of the research in a town with a population of about 23,000 commented: 'If you've got one member on the Council – and we've got twenty-two councillors – he can be swamped in vote, standing outside we have 600 or 700 individuals and this carries more weight than one councillor crying as a voice in the wilderness.'

The social class composition of the population of a particular locality and the size of the local authority it is served by are important 'background factors' which influence the development of ratepayer and similar movements in local politics. However, to understand why these movements developed in some areas and not in others one has to examine local patterns of conflict which may divide individuals who share the same views about national politics.

The 'expanding area'

Political conflict is likely to occur in localities which are undergoing a rapid increase of population because of an influx of immigrants from other areas for the following reasons:

1. There would appear to be a general tendency in human societies for conflict to occur between 'established' and 'outsider' groups. Such tensions are particularly likely to occur when the 'established' group is a closely-knit, 'traditional' community with an interlocking network of family and communal ties; and when the 'established' group see themselves as a superior social group and fear status degradation as a result of the influx of newcomers. [19] Scott Donaldson uses words such as 'inevitable', 'invariable' and 'ubiquitous' to discuss the likelihood of conflict in older communities which undergo an influx of a large number of newcomers. [20] However, it may be argued that a number of alternative political outcomes are in fact possible.

The first possibility is that the influx of a large number of incomers into a community will produce neither social nor political conflict. Crichton paints at least an approximation of a rural idyll in her description of a rapidly expanding Berkshire village in which the middle class incomers, at any rate, appear to have been successfully absorbed into village life. [21] In their study of a rural community in upstate New York, Vidich and Bensman suggest a number of reasons why newcomers may be successfully integrated into a community without undue tension. [22] Newcomers may perform a function within the community by carrying out tasks which existing groups are unable, or see themselves as unable to carry out – for example, successfully manipulating relationships with the outside world. In addition, broker groups may mediate between the incomers and hostile established groups, and incomer groups may be socially isolated and therefore do not come into conflict with other groups in the community.

The second possibility is that there will be social but not political conflict — for example, a Hertfordshire village discussed by Pahl was split down the middle along mutually reinforcing geographical and social lines, but these differences apparently did not reproduce themselves in any overt form in local politics. [23] This may have been because the village was in a rural district, and therefore the political stakes may not have been high enough to encourage local party formation; or perhaps the geographical isolation of the two groups was an inhibiting factor. Also, the development of the middle-class housing area seems to have been a gradual — and therefore probably less threatening — process. The fact that the established group was largely working class may have lessened the chances of it organising itself politically. In certain situations, the fact that one of the groups is too socially disorganised to defend effectively its interests by political means may be the main reason why conflict in everyday relationships does not spread to the political arena. [24]

The third general possibility is that social conflict will be expressed in local political life. This may happen in two alternative ways. First, conflict may be expressed through the local branches of the national political parties. Stacey's Banbury will serve as an example, although it should be emphasised that the division between old and new which she discusses in her first study of Banbury is not one between Banburian and immigrant as much as between traditionalist and non-traditional element in the life of the town. Not only was the Labour Party non-traditional to the town, but most of its active members were immigrants to the town. Problems of immigrant assimilation were contained within the opposition of traditionalism to non-traditionalism, which found political expression through the local opposition of Labour and the Conservative and Liberal parties.

Alternatively, either the 'established' group or the 'incomer' group may organise a 'genuine local party'. On the whole, it is rather unusual for 'established' groups to organise themselves in this way, as they tend to be well represented on the local council. However, sometimes such organisation may be seen to be necessary as a response to the political activities of an 'incomer' group. For example, Lyme Regis in Dorset developed 'Progressive' and 'Preservationist' parties when it was a separate local authority before reorganisation. The Lyme Regis Society, more generally referred to as the 'Preservationists', was the first group to be formed and drew much of its support from retired people. The Lyme Regis Progressive Society was formed 'as an alternative to the Lyme Regis Society' with the aim of ensuring 'the economic and social development of the town'. The organisers of the Progressive Society stated that 'they realised that there were many retired people who wanted Lyme Regis to stay as it was' but 'businessmen had to make a living in the town and visitors had to be encouraged'. [26]

2. Apart from hostility between 'established' and 'incomer' groups, the inability of the authorities to expand facilities such as schools in a rapidly developing area at a rate sufficient to meet the demand for them may create a political agitation for

remedies which expresses itself in the formation of a local party. The existence of this kind of problem was an important factor in the formation of the Penn Ratepayers' Association discussed by Jones. [27]

3. Particularly if they follow managerial or professional occupations, the incomers may resent being governed by an established leadership group made up of 'the butcher, the baker, and the candlestick maker' [28] to quote a statement issued by a Residents' Association in an expanding town.

4. The social situation in new housing areas may favour the formation of agitational organisations. People may use local associations to speed friendship formation, and the existence of shared grievances provides an acceptable motive for participating in residents' groups. For example, in his account of the development of residents' associations in new housing areas in pre-war suburban London, Jackson notes, 'For those fond of organising others, or of giving vent to their aggression in public action, there existed in almost every new area a residents' or ratepayers' association . . . (The associations) generally established a basis for social coherence in the absence of any other influence.' [29]

5. Many expanding towns (particularly those around London) have a large proportion of their population commuting to work by train. Some students of suburban politics argue that commuting has no sociological significance. [30] Others contend that it does have an impact on patterns of local social and political activity, but disagree about the nature, strength and direction of the impact. Basically, there are two schools of thought on the impact of commuting on local communities. The first of these schools of thought argues that extensive commuting to work by a large proportion of the local community tends to reduce participation in local organisations. [31] Two variants of this theme are stressed in the literature. The first of these argues that the number of hours spent commuting and the generally exhausting nature of the activity tends to discourage commuters from taking an interest in local organisations after they have reached home. The second argument which is put forward is that commuters have commitments to two different communities — their place of work and their place of residence. Their loyalties will be divided and any time they decide to devote to participation in public affairs will be split between the two communities to which they have a commitment. It is, of course, possible that they will have a 'negative' image of their place of work and a 'positive' image of their place of residence and that they will tend to 'compensate' for the time spent away from home by a high level of participation in local activities.

The argument that commuting does have a positive effect on local political activity is most cogently stated by Durant. [32] In her study of the Watling Estate in North London, she points out that the early morning workmen's train functioned as a common meeting ground for the men of the estate. The men who lived in the same street got to know each other in going to and returning from the station. The contacts made in this way provided the social basis for the subsequent formation of a Residents' Association.

The conditions of commuting may constitute a shared grievance which can be pursued by a residents' association. Jackson notes that the railway was a favourite target for the attention of residents' associations in pre-war London; for example, the Stoneleigh Residents' Association 'carried on almost continuous skirmishing with the Southern Railway Company . . . A major grumble was the inclusion in all trains of little-used First Class accommodation, another the inconsistent amounts of Third Class seating available'. [33] Similarly, 'Travel up 3rd class on the train' was a frequent cry at public meetings organised by the post-war Billericay Residents' Association discussed in the next chapter. Commuting by train may add to the pool of grievances on which a 'genuine local party' in an expanding town can draw.

A special type of 'established versus outsider' conflict occurs in parts of the central area of large cities. The process starts when middle class families start buying up and converting run-down properties formerly occupied by working class families. Gradually, the character of the area changes as the middle class newcomers move in alongside the long-standing working class residents.

A specific example is the Barnsbury area of Islington. Professional families started moving into the area in the late 1950s and early 1960s, and in 1965 a group of these families formed the Barnsbury Association. They persuaded the authorities to prepare an overall environmental plan for the area, but an interim report published in 1966 fell far short of the Barnsbury Association's hopes. In 1968, it successfully elected three 'Barnsbury Independents' to the Islington Council.

In the national data, it was found that there was a statistically significant but weak positive relationship between the rate of population expansion over the period studied and 'genuine local party' strength. This relationship held when a non-manual control was introduced. In the case of the Devon data, there was no statistically significant relationship between rate of population change and the mean share of the vote obtained by 'genuine local parties', but there was a significant relationship between the rate of population change and 'genuine local party' activity ($r = .3$). This relationship suggests that such movements were not electorally successful in rapidly expanding areas over the period studied; one of the problems is that Devon as a county contains fewer rapidly expanding areas than other parts of the country. A residents' association formed on a large new estate on the outskirts of a Devon town was examined as part of the study. The matters dealt with by the Association in its first year of existence offer a catalogue of the types of problem faced by residents in a rapidly expanding area — paths not made up, new development obscuring a view, the need for a local health centre, mobile library, community centre and more telephone kiosks. However, the Association felt that it could exert more influence as a pressure group outside the council.

Thus, the social and political conflicts which develop in rapidly expanding communities may find an expression through the local branches of the national political parties; they may lead to the formation of a ratepayers' or residents' movement which does not contest local elections; or, in some cases, they may lead to the formation of a 'genuine local party'. One such case is discussed in detail in the next chapter.

The resort town

The second general case is that of the resort town. As suggested by Smith in his study of Torquay, conflicts are likely to occur in such communities between residents who have no interest in the holiday industry, and the hotelier and trader interests who wish to support the industry's development by rate-financed municipal enterprise. A further important factor in the situation in such communities is the presence of large numbers of retired people who have moved to the resort at the end of their working lives. It is possible to exaggerate the proportion of retired people who make moves of this kind. A national sample survey carried out for Age Concern found that 'the proportion of elderly who move a long distance after retirement is quite small. Our total sample of 2,700 people showed only 183 people (7 per cent) have moved over fifty miles from their previous homes during the past ten years.' [34] However, some resorts are more attractive to individuals who make this kind of move than others. For example, in the South West of England (a popular area for retirement), 37 per cent of 'additional retireds' are to be found in the Exeter—Torbay area of Devon. [35]

Three general types of problem common to resort towns may contribute to the development of local political conflicts in these communities:

1. Ordinary residents tend to resent the expenditure of rate income on the provision of tourist facilities, whilst hotelier/trader interests tend enthusiastically to back such expenditures. This conflict is likely to be particularly acute in resorts with a large concentration of retired people. Their general 'rates consciousness' may focus on this particular area of expenditure.

2. The threat posed to amenity and property values by such unsightly facilities as caravan sites, car parks etc. may engender conflict.

3. Many residents are likely to resent the congestion of facilities which they normally use as a result of the annual invasion of holidaymakers. [36]

The actual focus of the conflict will vary from town to town. The actual issues may appear quite trivial to the outsider. For example, in one town the free admission of wives of conference delegates to municipal facilities became an issue; in another town, the fate of six illuminated gnomes was a source of controversy.

An additional factor is that political disputes in resort communities may encompass elements of 'established and outsider' conflicts. For example, in one Devon town ratepayers' association opponents of a proposal to spend the product of a halfpenny rate on resort publicity were castigated as 'aliens and newcomers'. [37] In general, newcomers in resort towns tend to be middle class retirees and it is argued that those resort towns which are also popular retirement communities will be particularly prone to conflicts between traders and ratepayer movements. As Kammerer points out, 'One of the chief mental characteristics of retirees is a "set" or attitude produced by the realisation that they will never again earn more income. No matter how high a pension or rentier income may be, the retirees become acutely tax and government conscious.' [38] They are therefore particularly likely to react with hostility to rate increases they see as resulting from the political pressures of tourist trade interests. As a group, they are particularly likely to resent the 'invasion' of the town by tourists, in so far as it brings with it noise and 'undesirables'.

The concentration of retired persons in resort communities leads to intensive social interaction among them, thus providing a basis for effective political mobilisation. They tend to develop a dense network of social relationships, both on an informal, personal basis and through organisations such as bridge clubs, bowls clubs and pensioner associations. For example, in a number of Devon resorts with large retired populations there are social clubs which appeal specifically to the middle class retired person with a programme of lectures, talks and discussions. In the event of a political crisis (such as a sharp rate increase), rapid word-of-mouth communication is relatively easy. [39]

Despite their relative poverty, retired persons in resorts are generally well endowed with political resources. A person who can afford (or would think of) retiring to a resort will generally have occupied a job in which he will have acquired organisational and other relevant skills. Apart from a few limited council schemes, retirement to a resort is effectively only an option open to owner-occupiers. The increased proportion of manual workers who are now owner-occupiers may eventually be reflected in the proportions of migrants who are of non-manual and manual origin. As it is, in the major retirement areas of the south-west, 'there is a very marked imbalance between the professional and managerial groups and the manual groups'. [40]

Perhaps more importantly, retirees are particularly well endowed with one key political resource — time. Indeed, having left behind old friends in their former place of residence, retirees in a resort community may find that time weighs heavily on their hands and be only too willing to assist in an organisation in which they will be fighting for relevant goals, and in which they will have the chance to make new friends. Kammerer et al. note that pensioners constitute a problem in many retirement towns where they spend their time scolding the council on minor matters. They report that minor procedures which go off smoothly in a town with a younger population cause considerable uproar in retirement communities. [41] In such towns, the extent of retiree participation in the town's affairs may itself become the subject of political dispute.

The political situation of retirees in a resort community may usefully be summarised in terms of a resources-opportunities-motivation paradigm. Because of their middle class background, they are well endowed with key *resources* such as speaking ability and organisational skills. The amount of time they have at their disposal provides them with the *opportunity* to engage in political activity. Their desire to limit rates expenditure and exclude 'undesirables' provides the necessary *motivation*.

Of course, age and ill health may have effects contrary to those discussed. A study of a Devon retirement community found that among those interviewed over the age of seventy-five, four out of five could no longer manage all the basic chores of daily life unaided. [42] Some social gerontologists [43] have suggested that independent of the effects of declining health and poverty, the aged person undergoes a process of 'disengagement' from the social system. The individual 'prepares' for death by disengaging from activity and society prepares him for the last stage of life by withdrawing its integrating pressures. However, after a prolonged and vigorous controversy during what have been termed social gerontology's 'disengagement years', it is now generally accepted that disengagement is 'just one possible pathway within one general solution to the challenge of ageing'. [44] After a cross-national study specifically designed to test the hypotheses of disengagement theory. Shannas *et alia.* concluded that their data did not suggest that 'independent of growing infirmity, disengagement is a widespread phenomenon'. [45]

Apart from the limited utility of disengagement theory as an explanation of the behaviour of the aged population in general, it should be remembered that retired persons in resort communities are likely to differ in their characteristics and behaviour from the pensioned population of the country as a whole. In particular, they are likely to include a disproportionately large number of 'early retirers' who are less likely to be afflicted by infirmity and ill health. In the south-west of Britain 'prematurely retired account for one-eight or more of the region's additional retired males' [46] and it was found that early retirement was particularly concentrated in the more popular retirement areas. American researchers have suggested that pensioners in retirement communities are more likely to evolve a satisfactory pattern of adjustment to retirement than the pensioned population as a whole. [47] This is not, of course, to say that there are not many socially isolated people in British retirement communities. A recent study of Ilfracombe in North Devon found that of 649 pensioners interviewed, 266 were living alone and 130 were unable to look after themselves because of disability. [48] However, when one is considering the likelihood of the formation of retiree-based ratepayer movements in resort communities, one has to remember that a relatively small group of activists is needed to form and sustain such a movement. Such activists may be drawn from the younger, more energetic and more outward-looking retirees; it should not be too difficult for them to persuade other, less active retirees that they have common interests.

A more precise specification of the relationship between the number of retirees in a resort and the occurrence of 'genuine local party' activity may be developed with reference to Rosow's work on the social integration of the aged. Although Rosow's field work was carried out in apartment buildings in Cleveland, and not in a geographically distinct retirement community, he sets out a coherent theory of the consequences of geographical age segregation. As a result of his empirical research, Rosow found that, 'Independently of social class, the confinement of friendships within the age group is disproportionately higher in high-density areas than in low-density areas (in terms of proportion of aged) . . . The larger the potential friendship field, the less likely are old people even to look for alternatives, to seek out or accept younger friendships.' [49] Rosow suggests that these findings indicate 'a definite "tipping point" where the concentration of old people orients them more significantly to their age peers'. [50] He stresses that, 'The relationship between the local concentration and social activity of old people is not strictly linear, but increases disproportionately to concentration. There is a threshold effect in which minimally half the dwelling units in a residential setting must have an older person before strong neighbouring patterns are stimulated and interaction is significantly intensified.' [51]

Rosow is able to trace a link between the number of retirees living in a particular locality and certain aspects of their social behaviour. However, he does not make any explicit predictions about the effect of the higher levels of social interaction found in areas with high concentrations of retirees on patterns of political activity. The fact that concentration affects social behaviour does not necessarily mean that political behaviour will in turn be affected. In order to argue that local political activity is so affected, it will be necessary to add another link to the chain of causal explanation.

There are a number of reasons why the non-linear relationship between the number of aged persons in a locality and patterns of social activity may carry through to political life. Rosow suggests on the basis of his empirical findings that old people in settings of high residential concentration 'are more likely than others to know personally old people whom they greatly admire'. [52] Old people who are admired by other retirees in this way are favourably placed to act as political leaders should a need for the adoption of such a role be perceived to arise. When one takes into account the other factors which have been mentioned, such as the fact that retirees are relatively well endowed with political resources, it does not seem unreasonable to hypothesise that, given a suitable trigger action, their presence in large numbers in a particular community may lead to the formation of a 'genuine local party'. It should be added that many retirees apparently do not perceive activity of this sort as 'political', but rather as an extension of the kind of 'community activity' similar to belonging to a retiree social club or local cultural organisation.

As in the case of 'expanding areas', it is not suggested that all resort towns will have local parties. In some resorts, certain factors which may help to mitigate conflict between residents and traders may be present. Two major factors of this type can be discerned: geographical segregation of resort activities, and resort specialisation.

In larger towns, it is possible to confine noisy resort activities to a particular small area of the town. This area 'can be fairly well defined and a concentration of "fun" develops'. [53] In the smaller resorts, however, this is not a feasible strategy and a policy choice then has to be made between annoying residents and depriving the resort of evening entertainment.

Some resorts — large and small — concentrate on a particular section of the holiday market. In part, this type of resort specialisation is an economic strategy; however, it can also be employed as a political conflict-reduction mechanism. For example, at Budleigh Salterton in Devon, the town has developed, '(a) limited, quiet resort function, main provision being for resident retired population. This has been made possible by unusual land-owning conditions. The result seems to be a social organisation based on retired leisure which older people find very satisfying.' [54]

However, not every resort can appeal to the 'select' or 'quiet' section of the market which is likely to meet with retiree approval. For example, at one Cornish resort the encouragement of an 'artistic' image attracted a number of so-called 'hippies' to the town. This in turn led to serious conflicts in the town which, on occasion, 'brought some people to the edge of mob violence'. [55]

In the national aggregate data analysis, it was found that there was a weak positive relationship between 'resort status' (treated as a 'dummy variable') [56] and 'genuine local party' strength. When a non-manual control was introduced, it was found that among local authorities with a low non-manual component in their populations, the relationship between resort status and 'genuine local party' strength no longer held. However, among the local authorities with a relatively high non-manual component in their populations, there was a highly significant relationship between resort status and 'genuine local party' strength.

Analysis of the Devon data showed that there was a positive and moderately strong correlation between the percentage of retired males in the ward and the 'genuine local party' share of the vote ($r = .35$) and 'genuine local party' activity ($r = .33$). Similar results were obtained when the percentage of pensioners and resort status was used as the independent variable although, of course, all three variables are highly intercorrelated.

Rosow's notion of a 'tipping point' beyond which social interaction among old people is intensified would seem to have some applicability to the study of their political behaviour in English resort communities, although the 'threshold effect' seems to take place at a rather lower level than that anticipated by Rosow in relation to social activity:

Table 2.1

Pensioners and 'genuine local party' activity in Devon, 1955-68

Percentage of seats contested by 'genuine local parties' (excluding tenant parties) over period	Percentage of persons of pensionable age in ward (1966 census data)		
	less than 20%	20–29%	Over 30%
None	45% (9)	51% (28)	32% (7)
0–19%	55% (11)	33% (18)	27% (6)
Over 20%	–	16% (9)	41% (9)
	100%	100%	100%

It is apparent from the above table that both the occurrence and the regularity of 'genuine local party' intervention increased in wards with large concentrations of retired persons, with the 'tipping point' being around the thirty per cent level.

Many 'genuine local parties', particularly in resorts, called themselves ratepayers' associations and emphasised the level of the rates as a key issue. It was therefore decided to explore the relationship between changes in the level of rates levied by a local authority and the incidence of 'genuine local party' activity. It quickly became apparent that 'genuine local party' activity was not a simple function of a high county ranking in Devon in terms of rate poundage or rate call per head. For example, seventy-five per cent of the wards situated in resort towns which had rankings of nineteen or above in the county rate poundage league table in more than two-thirds of the years between 1955 and 1966 experienced 'genuine local party' activity in that period (N = 36). The comparable percentage for non-resort wards with similar rankings was only seventeen per cent. (N = 24). If one considers the wards situated in resort towns which had rankings of nineteen or above in the rate poundage per head county table in more than five-sixths of the years between 1955 and 1966, eighty-three per cent experienced 'genuine local party' activity in that period (N = 42). The comparable percentage for non-resort wards with similar ratings was only seventeen per cent. (N = 24).

The introduction of county ranking in terms of rate call per head as an intervening variable led to an improvement in the correlations obtained between the key independent and dependent variables: [57]

Table 2.2
Independent variable

	'Genuine local party' mean share of vote	'Genuine local party' activity
Percentage pensioners	.41	.25
Resort status	.62	.30
		N = 66

The general conclusion which is drawn is that 'genuine local parties' are particularly likely to form in resort towns with large retirement communities, but that the likelihood of such parties forming — and in particular the propensity of electors to vote for them — may be affected by higher than average rate calls per head.

Major disputes over a town's future

Major disputes over a town's future represent the only one of the situations discussed in which the *trigger action* is likely to create *underlying sustaining factors*. In other words, the trigger action raises issues of such an important kind that it creates entirely new lines of division in a community. An example would be an announcement that a town is to be considered as a 'reception area' for 'overspill development'. This would obviously raise important questions of a 'what kind of town shall ours be?' type, and prolonged conflict, including the formation of local parties, is likely to ensue. The controversy over proposed overspill development in Barnstaple, Devon, is an example.

Tenant parties

Some tenant parties may develop in response to the type of 'expanding area' situation discussed earlier. Indeed, the arguments of the proponents of the 'phase hypothesis' that tenants' associations are most likely to be successful in the first three to six months of an estate's life is a persuasive one. Later, as the initial requests for amenities are met, matters of common interest tend to appear less frequently and matters of individual interest more frequently. [58]

Whilst the importance of the tenant role as a determinant of behaviour undoubtedly lessens as residents on a new estate settle down, it may be questioned whether the interests shared by residents in a given locality are invariably 'few and weak' thereafter. [59] Brier and Dowse have shown that an unpopular decision by a local council which threatens a large group of tenants may re-activate feelings of group solidarity and a tenants' party may be formed. [60]

However, because of certain problems which are peculiar to council housing estates, local parties are likely to arise on them only under specially favourable circumstances. These problems may be summarised as follows:

1. Social and political leadership skills are generally less widely available among working class as opposed to middle class populations. Whilst foremen and junior non-manual workers often live on council housing estates, they are often unwilling to associate with their neighbours for status reasons. In a comparative study of a Liverpool and a Sheffield housing estate, it was concluded that: '. . . The survival of a measure of community organisation on the Liverpool estate, in contrast to its disappearance at Sheffield, appears to be due in large measure to the existence on the former of potential leaders whose status was high enough to enable them to be recognised and accepted, but not so high as to make it impossible for them to associate informally with other members of the group.' [61]

2. The absence of common traditions of behaviour may inhibit social communication. Elias and Scotson note in their study of the estate at 'Winston Parva' that 'the different local traditions which families carried with them on their migration as part of their personal make-up created misunderstandings . . . There was a lack of common customs of co-operation and of common rituals of social intercourse generally which in older communities served as lubricants of human relations.' [62]

3. Often estates are split against themselves, with two or more distinct antagonistic social sections, the people in the supposedly 'better' section displaying a considerable degree of contempt for the rest. For example, on a council estate in Cardiff, people living on the top of the hill were reported to look down (socially) on those living in the geographically lower areas. [63]

4. Tenant grievances are normally articulated through the Labour Party. One would only expect independent tenant organisation when a Labour council group fails to satisfactorily discharge its role of tenants' guardian. An additional problem is that very often most of the tenants on a particular estate with leadership skills are already involved in the Labour Party organisation. Indeed, some of the most electorally successful tenant movements before local government reorganisation were in areas where the Labour Party had traditionally been weak (e.g., Honiton and Exmouth in Devon, Ely in East Anglia). [64]

Tenants' organisations would seem to be particularly likely to be formed when a rent increase is accompanied by some alteration in the structure of the rent assessment system which threatens a cherished value widely held by tenants. In Exeter, a rent differential was proposed based on household income, including levies on lodgers, children over the age of eighteen not receiving full time education, and wife's income. According to Brier and Dowse, 'the most important single determinant' of the action of the executive of the Tenants' Association that was subsequently formed was 'a strong feeling of outrage'. [65] This feeling of outrage 'apparently centred around the concept of privacy. The tenants' leaders felt very strongly indeed about the incursion of the political into what they considered was the private. By this they meant that wives' earnings and detailed information about bonus and overtime working was something that the individual was entitled to have remain a secret.' [66]

Similarly, in the case of a tenants' movement in Sheffield, there was 'a deep emotional objection to the declaration of income that would be necessary when applying for a (rent) rebate'. [67] In particular, 'the most contentious part of the rent scheme was the adult occupiers' surcharge . . . The surcharge was payable by adult children of the tenant and evoked great emotional opposition from the tenants who interpreted the proposal as an attack on the unity of the family.' [68] On the whole, however, relatively few tenant movements have successfully contested elections.

Finally, consideration will be given to four less important sets of circumstances in which 'genuine local parties' may develop. On occasions, middle class radicals may be sufficiently offended by a local authority's decisions to intervene in local politics. For example, the 'Save Leamington Action Movement' contested the last borough council elections in Leamington, Warwickshire, before local government reorganisation on a conservationist platform. Describing the 'SLAM' campaign, the local newspaper remarked of its candidates, 'Living in Regency houses, the four are possessed, perhaps, of something of the spa-town spirit not yet quite departed from a place with a Royal prefix.' [69] None of the four candidates were successful, although the presence of a 'SLAM' candidate in one ward may have contributed to the surprise defeat of the Conservatives by a narrow margin. SLAM's original slogan was 'We Like Leamington'. However, in general, middle class radicals are generally cosmopolitan in their outlook, and as Parkin points out, 'Local politics with its emphasis on pragmatic and practical matters is obviously the sphere least liable to attract the interest of those disposed to politics as an expressive activity.' [70]

Sometimes, the stimulus of a sharp rate increase may be sufficient to lead to the formation of a *ratepayers' party,* even when underlying sustaining factors of the type discussed are not present in the local political system. However, prior to reorganisation, such parties were not particularly successful when underlying sustaining factors were absent. [71] The rate revaluation controversy of the early 1960's led to the formation of a number of parties of the 'Ratepayer' type, but these parties seem to have survived primarily in the specially favoured political environments of the type outlined. However, 'genuine local parties' of this type have become more significant in the wake of the large rate increases following reorganisation and they will be discussed more fully in Chapter Four.

In areas with large populations drawn from minority ethnic groups, local parties may emerge purporting to represent a *particular ethnic group* in the community. [72] Lastly, a serious split in a national political party in a particular community may lead to the formation of a new party which contests elections; the most striking examples are Lincoln, where the Democratic Labour Party won control and Blyth, where Independent Labour candidates gained a significant number of seats. Of course, *defecting partisans* are not a new feature of British local politics. There are countless examples of councillors who have left their party for one reason or another and stood for re-election as independents or under such labels as 'True Labour' or 'Real Labour'. Most of these defectors have been consigned to political oblivion. Blyth and Lincoln are important but exceptional cases. They are different from the 'genuine local parties' discussed in this book since they represent a spillover from an essentially national political conflict into local politics.

Alternative political outcomes

It has already been pointed out that the conflicts described in the analytical framework may lead to the formation of ratepayer and similar movements which confine themselves to 'pressure group' activities and do not contest elections. Two other alternative political outcomes need to be discussed; the conduct of conflict through 'independents' in a 'nonpartisan' local political system; and the articulation of grievances through the Liberal Party.

Ratepayer groups generally emphasise their opposition to party politics in local government, but often they represent the most organised form of political activity in nonpartisan systems. Sometimes, however, the kinds of conflicts which are endemic in (say) resorts may be conducted through less organised groups. For example, at the 1970 urban district council elections in Budleigh Salterton, Devon, three candidates fought as a loosely organised 'slate' of independents 'under the banner of giving Budleigh Salterton a younger look'. [73] They were opposed by a slate of candidates who favoured the 'status quo'. Thus the conflict about Salterton's image of 'being run by a few elderly people' [74] was fought without the formation of local parties but rather through more informal and *ad hoc* arrangements.

The types of local conflict situation which have been discussed may, in certain circumstances, lead to a resurgence of Liberalism in a particular locality rather than the emergence of new local political parties. In his analysis of local political parties, Steed suggests that 'there is some evidence that the Ratepayer vote is in some part a substitute Liberal vote'. [75] Young has suggested 'that the challenge to the local establishment in Orpington might well have taken the form of a "ratepayer" movement had not the small band of resident Liberals been ready and able to channel dissent in a more avowedly political direction'. [76]

Clearly, Steed's statement is open to a number of interpretations. It may be taken simply to mean that voters wishing to register a protest against government policies will vote for the candidate of a 'genuine local party' when no Liberal candidate is available. It is certainly true that Liberal candidates experienced an upsurge in popularity in council elections at about the same time as the candidates of local political movements, but whereas the number of Liberal councillors began to decline rapidly after 1963, the number of 'genuine local party' councillors continued to increase. This trend suggests that electoral support for local parties is something more than an ephemeral gesture of disgust at the actions of the government in office.

An alternative interpretation of Steed's hypothesis is that local political parties of the ratepayer type and Liberal parties in local politics tend to draw their support from similar socio-political environments, and that the local discontents which find expression through ratepayer and tenant associations may alternatively find expression through the local Liberal party. It may be suggested that the Liberal Party has a number of characteristics which make it more likely that it will become a vehicle of local political protest than the other national parties.

Sharpe has pointed out that 'The Liberal Party . . . cannot be viewed as a unified party in anything like the same sense as the other two major parties'. [77] Lacking a national base linked with a producer interest which provides an ideological consistency, its character depends 'as much on the personalities who must undertake the drudgery of continuous local organisation, and the local political context in which this takes place, as on party doctrine and policy as laid down by the national party'. [78]

In addition, it has been suggested that Liberal distrust of central direction and national headquarter's lack of funds have combined to give local party organisations a greater degree of autonomy than is possessed by their counterparts in the Conservative or Labour parties. [79] As Birch tersely puts it, 'Liberalism is a cause which has been described in rather different ways in different parts of the country'. [80]

Because of their 'localism', Liberal parties may emerge as local protest movements similar to those who cloak themselves in the organisational device of, say, a ratepayers' association. A particular local decision may evoke indignation, one of a group of protesters may have Liberal sympathies, and the Liberal bandwagon may appear an attractive one on which to climb — a useful vehicle of protest combining an absence of local 'strings' with the possibility of national assistance.

It is not argued that Liberal strength is simply a function of local discord. Clearly, there are factors which help to explain the distribution of Liberal strength in the country as a whole which are of little or no importance for the purely local movements which have been discussed in this chapter. The prospect of the next general election gives Liberals a 'sustaining incentive' which does not exist in the case of the purely local party. This may be why Liberal parties often enjoy a somewhat longer span of life than the generally ephemeral local party.

The national aggregate data showed an extremely weak and statistically insignificant positive relationship between 'genuine local party' and Liberal strength. To a limited degree, this finding lends some support to the 'substitute vote' hypothesis; if voting for a 'genuine local party' is a substitute for voting Liberal, one would not expect to find a good 'genuine local party' performance in terms of winning seats to be strongly correlated with good Liberal performance in winning seats. However, the existence of a strong negative relationship between 'genuine local party' strength and Liberal strength would lend even stronger support to the 'substitute vote' hypothesis. The results are rather inconclusive; the absence of a strong positive correlation means that 'substitute voting' cannot be entirely discounted, but equally the absence of a strong negative correlation suggests that it is not a widespread phenomenon.

In Scotland and Wales, voting Nationalist may be an alternative to voting for a ratepayer candidate. Butt Phillip suggests that, in the case of Wales, 'there is evidence that votes for Plaid Cymru in local elections are interchangeable with votes for Ratepayer candidates'. [81] This hypothesis seemed to receive some support from the results of the 1976 local government elections in South Wales; there was a tendency for either Ratepayer candidates or the Plaid to win seats from Labour in particular districts. For example, Plaid Cymru won control of Merthyr from Labour, winning one Ratepayer seat in the process; the Ratepayers won control of Swansea from Labour with Plaid Cymru winning only one seat.

The impact of local government reorganisation

The analytical framework discussed in this chapter was developed to explain the incidence and success of purely local political parties before local government reorganisation. Local government reorganisation has had a number of important consequences for the pattern of activity of such movements. Consider the two main categories discussed in the analytical framework, the rapidly expanding area and the resort town. Apart from the fact that there were fewer rapidly expanding areas in the mid-1970's as the rate of private house building slowed down, movements in such areas faced a changed set of circumstances which were likely to affect their calculations about whether or not they should follow an electoral strategy. Reorganisation produced councils covering larger areas with (in the majority of cases) more councillors. As has been pointed out, under the old system, particularly in the smaller urban districts and non-county boroughs, a ratepayers' organisation could reasonably hope to win a substantial proportion of seats on the council. There is much less hope of this happening on a larger authority. Even before reorganisation, many ratepayer movements were reluctant to contest elections. The effects of reorganisation are likely to increase this reluctance.

The aggregate analysis showed that 'genuine local parties' were most likely to be successful in resorts forming an urban district or non-county borough with a population of under 100,000. However, this type of local political system has been largely swept away by reorganisation (although there are exceptions, such as Worthing, which has an electorally successful ratepayers' movement). In the smaller resort authorities, there was often a delicate balance of power between retired residents and traders. However, most resorts have now been incorporated in larger districts which include urban towns and/or substantial rural areas often represented by individuals who are as hostile to the tourist trade as retirees. In many cases, expenditure on advertising resorts etc. has been substantially cut, although in Cornwall the battle continues at a county level with the ratepayers' federation calling for the abolition of the Cornwall Tourist Board and the sacking of its staff.

A further consequence of reorganisation (although one has to stress that general inflation played a major, if not the larger, part) was a rapid increase in the level of rates in many areas, particularly in towns on the fringe of urban areas which were incorporated into new authorities. This led to the formation of a number of new ratepayer protest movements in rather different socio-political environments from those described in this chapter (for example, in urban areas in the West Midlands and the North of England). It is therefore concluded that the analytical framework developed in this chapter, however adequate for the period before reorganisation, needs to be modified to take account of the substantial changes in the pattern of local government and politics since 1974. A modified analytical framework is presented in a later chapter.

Notes

[1] The title of this chapter is adapted from K. Young, *Essays on the Study of Urban Politics,* Macmillan, London 1975, where he exorts researchers in the area of local politics to 'study the unusual'.

[2] J. Stanyer, *Understanding Local Government,* Fontana, London 1976, p.82.

[3] Ibid., p.82.

[4] M. Steed, 'Ratepayers Associations and Local Politics', *Insight,* June 1965, pp. 11–16, p.12.

[5] A.J. Beith, 'An Anti-Labour Caucus: The Case of the Northumberland Voters' Association', *Policy and Politics,* vol.2, no.2, 1974, pp. 153–165, p.163.

[6] Ibid., p.155.

[7] B. Elliott, D. McCrone, V. Skelton, 'Property and Political Power: Edinburgh 1875 to 1975', p.14. Mimeographed paper, Department of Sociology, University of Edinburgh.

[8] R.V. Clements, *Local Notables and City Politics,* MacMillan, London 1969, p.21n.

[9] A number of studies of local politics contain references to movements of this kind, but there has not been a systematic attempt to investigate their origins and consequences.

[10] The national political climate may have some influence in creating conditions which are more or less favourable for the emergence of 'genuine local parties'.

[11] H.E. Bracey, *Neighbours*, Routledge, London 1964, p.91.

[12] The national data was obtained from *The Times* and the *Municipal Year Book*. For each of the local authorities studied, the total number of seats on the particular authority's council each May was aggregated for the period of the study (or for the period of existence of the authority during the period covered by the study), and the total number of seats (if any) held by 'genuine local parties' on the particular authority was similarly aggregated. The second figure was then expressed as a percentage of the first. Non-local minor parties (Nationalists, Communists etc.) and 'defecting partisans' (Independent Conservatives etc.) were excluded from these calculations. An operational distinction had to be made between 'concealed Conservative' parties and 'genuine local parties'. Parties were designated as 'concealed Conservative' — and therefore not as 'genuine local parties' — only when they clearly fulfilled that role: that is, when there were (a) no official Conservative on the particular council in a given year, and (b) no substantial group of independent councillors who might be 'concealed Conservatives', 'substantial' being defined as 'more than 12.5 per cent of the council as a whole, or three members, whichever is the greater'. It should be noted that the existence of the aldermanic system before reorganisation may have injected an element of confusion into the data for boroughs, as 'purely local parties' were often better represented among councillors than among aldermen. The Devon data was derived from material on election results in the county of Devon collected by J. Stanyer under the auspices of a Social Science Research Council grant; the relevant census data was processed by the author.

[13] W.P. Grant, *Independent Local Political Parties: The Origin, Development and Consequences of Ratepayer and Similar Groups*, Ph.D. thesis, University of Exeter, 1972.

[14] 'Non-manual' was defined in terms of the Registrar General's socio-economic groups, one to six plus thirteen.

[15] Royal Commission on Local Government in England, Research Studies 9, *Community Attitudes Survey: England*, HMSO, London 1969, p.164.

[16] J. Stanyer, 'Social and Rational Models of Man: Alternative Approaches to the Study of Local Elections', *The Advancement of Science*, vol.26, no.130, 1970, pp. 399–407, p.404.

[17] *Community Attitudes Survey*, op. cit., p.106.

[18] D. Berry, *The Sociology of Grass Roots Politics*, Macmillan, London 1970, p.34

[19] Both these conditions are fulfilled in the case study by N. Elias and J. Scotson, *The Established and the Outsiders*, Frank Cass, London 1965.

[20] S. Donaldson, *The Suburban Myth*, Columbia University Press, New York 1965, pp.53, 159, 161–3.

[21] R.M. Crichton, *Commuters' Village: a Study of Community and Commuters in the Berkshire Village of Stratford Mortimer*, Macdonald, London 1964, pp.61, 71–2, 88–9.

[22] A.J. Vidich and J. Bensman, *Small Town in Mass Society*, Doubleday Anchor, New York 1960.

[23] R.E. Pahl, 'Class and Community in English Commuter Villages', *Socialogia Ruralis*, vol. 5, no.1, 1965, pp. 5–23.

[24] As was the case in the estate in 'Winston Parva' studied by Elias and Scotson, op. cit.

[25] M. Stacey, *Tradition and Change: a Study of Banbury*, Oxford University Press, London 1961.

[26] *Pulman's Weekly News,* 12 May 1970.

[27] G.W. Jones, *Borough Politics*, Macmillan, London 1969, pp.207–14.

[28] From a statement issued by Billericay Residents' Association.

[29] A.A. Jackson, *Semi-Detached London*, Allen and Unwin, London 1973, p.184.

[30] See W.M. Dobriner, *Class in Suburbia*, Prentice-Hall, Englewood Cliffs N.J. 1973.

[31] See W.T. Martin, 'The Structuring of Social Relationships Engendered by Suburban Residence' in W.M. Dobriner (ed.), *The Suburban Community*, Putnam, New York 1958; A.H. Scaff, 'The Effect of Commuting on Participation in Community Organisation', *American Sociological Review*, vol.17, no.2, April 1952, pp. 215–20.

[32] R. Durant, *Watling: A Survey of Social Life on a New Housing Estate*, P.S. King, London 1939.

[33] Jackson, op.cit., p.286.

[34] *The Attitudes of the Retired and Elderly*, Age Concern, London 1974, p.16.

[35] South-West Economic Planning Council, *Retirement to the South West*, HMSO, London 1975, p.4.

[36] The trader-resident conflict over visitors is a long standing one. For an early statement of the arguments see the report of the debate of the 3rd reading of the Health Resorts and Watering Places Bill (11 June 1920), 139 H.C. Deb. 5s, columns 832–847. For a more recent catalogue of the grievances of residents of resorts in relation to visitors see R.F. Delderfield, *For My Own Amusement*, Hodder, London 1968.

[37] *Pulman's Weekly News,* 18 November 1969 and 25 November 1969.

[38] G.K. Kammerer, C.D. Farris, J.M. DeGreve, A.B. Clubok, *The Urban Political Community: Profiles in Town Politics*, Houghton Miffin, Boston 1963, p.115.

[39] Klapper suggests, 'That face-to-face persuasion is a far more effectual instrument of pedagogy and persuasion than any impersonal medium is the heavy consensus of opinion among social scientists and public opinion experts'. J.T. Klapper, 'The Comparative Effects of the Various Media' in W. Schramm (ed.), *The Processes and Effects of Mass Communication*, University of Illinois Press, Urbana 1954.

[40] South-West Economic Planning Council, op.cit., pp.5–6.

[41] Kammerer et al., op.cit., p.159.

[42] A. Glyn-Jones, *Growing Older in a South Devon Town*, Exeter University Press, Exeter 1975, p.xi.

[43] E. Cummings and W.E. Henry, *Growing Old: the Process of Disengagement,* Basic Books, New York 1961, represents the initial and major statement of disengagement theory.

[44] R. Kastenbaum, 'Theories of Human Ageing: the Search for a Conceptual Framework', *Journal of Social Issues,* vol.21, no.1, 1965, pp.13–35, p.33.

[45] E. Shannas, P. Townsend, D. Wedderburn, H. Friis, P. Milhoj, J. Stehouwer, *Old People in Three Industrial Societies,* Routledge, London 1968, p.442.

[46] South-West Economic Planning Council, op.cit., p.5.

[47] S. Granick, 'Personality Adjustment of the Aged in Retirement Communities', *Geriatrics,* 1957, pp.381–385.

[48] Reported in *The Guardian,* 2 March 1977.

[49] I. Rosow, *Social Integration of the Aged,* Collier-Macmillan, London 1967, p.75.

[50] Ibid., p.75.

[51] Ibid., p.74.

[52] I. Rosow, 'Old People: Their Friends and Neighbours', *American Behavioural Scientist,* vol.14, no.1, pp.59–69, p.64.

[53] F.M. Lewes, A.J. Culyer, G.A. Brady, *The Holiday Industry of Devon and Cornwall,* HMSO, London 1970, p.138.

[54] Ibid., p.200.

[55] *The Times,* 18 July 1969.

[56] That is to say, when the data was coded for computer analysis, non-resorts were quantified as 'O' and resorts as '1'. See H.R. Alker Jnr. *Mathematics and Politics,* Macmillan, London 1965, pp.81–87. A number of different ways of defining 'resort' were considered, but it was eventually decided to use a subjective listing. A similar procedure was used by Butler and Stokes in their study of *Political Change in Britain.* (Personal communication from David Butler, 13 November 1970.

[57] In the calculations used to produce this table, two towns in which the formation of 'purely local parties' had been the result of 'major disputes over a town's future' (Exeter and Barnstaple) were excluded from the analysis.

[58] R.N. Morris and J. Mogey, *The Sociology of Housing: Studies at Berinsfield,* Routledge, London 1965, pp. 62–3.

[59] N. Dennis, 'Changes in Function and Leadership Renewal', *Sociological Review,* N.S.9, no.1, 1961, pp. 55–84, p.62.

[60] A.P. Brier and R.E. Dowse, 'Political Mobilisation: a Case Study', *International Review of Community Development,* no.19–20, 1968, pp.327–40.

[61] M.W. Hodges and C.S. Smith, 'The Sheffield Estate' in *Neighbourhood and Community: an Enquiry into Social Relationships on Housing Estates in Liverpool and Sheffield,* University of Liverpool Press, Liverpool 1954, p.139.

[62] Elias and Scotson, op.cit., p.73.

[63] J. Tucker, *Honourable Estates,* Gollancz, London 1966, p.71.

[64] These tenant parties were not counted as 'genuine local parties' for the purposes of the aggregate analysis.

[65] Brier and Dowse, op.cit., p.333.

[66] Ibid., p.333.

[67] W. Hampton, *Democracy and Community: a Study of Politics in Sheffield*, Oxford University Press, London 1970, p.247.

[68] Ibid., p.262.

[69] *Coventry Evening Telegraph,* 28 April 1972.

[70] F. Parkin, *Middle Class Radicalism,* Manchester University Press, Manchester 1968, p.37.

[71] A good example is the Manchester Ratepayers' Party discussed by Bulpitt: J.G. Bulpitt, *Party Politics in English Local Government,* Longmans, London 1967, pp.73, 75.

[72] The so-called Bradford Branch of the Pakistan Peoples' Party may, in one sense, be regarded as a 'genuine local party'. M.J. Le Lohe, 'Participation in Elections by Asians in Bradford' in I. Crewe (ed.), *British Political Sociology Yearbook, Volume 2,* Croom Helm, London 1976, pp. 84–122, p.105.

[73] *Exmouth Journal,* 25 April 1970.

[74] *Exmouth Journal,* 9 May 1970.

[75] Steed, op.cit., p.14.

[76] K. Young, 'Orpington and the "Liberal Revival" ' in C. Cook and J. Ramsden (eds.), *By-Elections in British Politics,* Macmillan, London 1973, pp. 198–222, p.213.

[77] L.J. Sharpe, *Voting in Cities: the 1964 Borough Elections,* Macmillan, London 1967, p.9.

[78] Ibid., p.9.

[79] See J.S. Rasmussen, *The Liberal Party: a Study of Retrenchment and Revival,* Constable, London 1965, pp.86–7.

[80] A.H. Birch, *Small Town Politics,* Oxford University Press, London 1959, p.58.

[81] A. Butt Philip, *The Welsh Question,* University of Wales Press, Cardiff 1975, p.147.

3   Purely local politics

In the last chapter an attempt was made to develop an analytical framework which explained why ratepayers' and residents' movements were more successful in some areas than in others. Although each local political system is unique, it is possible to detect similar patterns of politics in districts which share similar socio-economic characteristics. By discussing specific cases, this chapter attempts to illustrate the patterns of politics which can develop in particular kinds of polity, e.g. the resort and the town with a rapidly expanding population. It also attempts to explore the ways in which the choices made by actors in a local political system may influence the development of that system in particular directions.

Certain kinds of local socio-economic environment tend to favour the development of ratepayer movements. However, not all resort towns (for example) have ratepayer movements. One must therefore consider the role of the 'sporadic interventionists' which bring such movements into being. There is a general assumption in much of the popular debate about local government that the lack of public interest in local government (as, for example, manifested by low turnout in local elections) is irrational. A contrary view is taken here; it is argued that the question that needs to be asked about local politics is not 'Why do so few people participate?' but 'Why do so many people participate?'

In his seminal discussion of voluntary organisations attempting to obtain collective or public goods (that is to say, benefits which must either be universally enjoyed or not enjoyed at all, but cannot be confined to particular individuals), Olson suggests that 'Unless the number of individuals in a group is quite small, or unless there is coercion or some other special device to make individuals act in their common interest, rational, self-interested individuals will not act to achieve their common or group interests'. [1] It is therefore necessary for large organisations to support their continued existence by 'providing some sanction or attraction distinct from the public good itself, that will lead individuals to help bear the burdens of maintaining the organisation'. [2]

It could be argued that in the case of ratepayer and similar movements, the motivation to participate is principally an altruistic one. Certainly, moral indignation is almost always present as an element in the pronouncements of ratepayer movements on local affairs. However, as Dowse and Hughes point out, 'Initially, those outraged appear almost euphoric about their chances of success, but the grind of mounting a campaign, presenting a detailed set of counter-proposals, or indeed comprising with those who have outraged them is a rather disillusioning process. Euphoria rapidly gives place to cynicism'. [3] Similarly, in his work on 'amateur Democrats' in the United States, Wilson points out, 'The moral fervour of the amateur generates considerable enthusiasm among the activists, transmutes politics into a "cause", and brings together people of similar class and educational background'. [4] However, these benefits of mobilising the 'amateur spirit' are outweighed by the fact that 'The amateur must constantly find ideals, personalities and causes sufficient to replenish the easily exhausted reservoir of enthusiasm which stimulates him'. [5] Even if new crusades are available, it is difficult to persuade activists to engage in sustained effort for the organisation. As Wilson points out, persuading activists 'to work several nights a week for two or three months of a campaign is difficult in itself, but persuading them to repeat the process in succeeding campaigns poses even greater problems'. [6]

In their study of political campaigning in the London parliamentary constituency of Barons Court, Holt and Turner suggest that 'since the local (constituency) party in a political campaign is a voluntary organisation and cannot effectively employ negative sanctions to stimulate its workers to greater and more effective activity, the basic incentive system must primarily involve a set of 'rewards' which many of the most active members seek'. [7] However, it is clear that many of the rewards available to the constituency branch of a national political party as disccused by Holt and Turner (qualification for a Parliamentary candidature through party work, the Honours List etc.) are not available to a local ratepayers' association.

One has to look for a rather different framework of analysis to account for the behaviour of individuals who become active in ratepayer and similar movements. As part of the research for this study, personal interviews were conducted with forty-five activists in ratepayer and similar movements. Whilst these interviews represent neither a large nor random sample of the considerable number of individuals involved in movements of these kinds, an analysis of the replies may add to our knowledge of an aspect of political activity which has not been studied in any depth. Of course, the majority of the activists themselves would deny that they are engaging in political activity (which they tend to equate with party activity). Many activists genuinely believe that they are, in some sense, expressing a general community will which transcends the sordid political objectives of the parties.

The first point that needs to be made is that many activists first join movements of this kind because they are asked; they are approached by a friend or a neighbour, or they attend the annual general meeting and are recruited on to the committee. However, one may presume that not everyone who is asked is willing to volunteer his services. For many respondents, the local ratepayer movement offered an opportunity to air grievances and an ability to influence local decisions. When they were asked why they agreed to help in the running of their association, respondents frequently made remarks like: 'When you see so many things which you feel are being messed up by local councillors who do not live in the area you feel it is the only way you can voice your opinions. It's a good outlet for one's feelings in a democratic way'.

The replies to the questionnaires suggest that the individuals who do volunteer to serve as activists often share a distinctive philosophy of life which predates their participation in a local ratepayer movement. A strong emphasis on the importance of self-help emerged from a number of the interviews. Respondents seemed to feel that the majority of citizens were too anxious to grumble and too unwilling to take positive action to attempt to remedy their complaints. In these circumstances, it was their duty to try to redress the balance:

> I like to think I am helping in some way. There is a lot of apathy. People prefer to let things go. Same with our union at work. The basic thing is that it is something more positive than just sitting about and moaning. Self-help.
>
> I thought I'd like to do something. You can just sit around all your life and do nothing. Might as well have a little try. Too many people sit around and let others do things for them.

This emphasis on helping others may be related to the fact that a relatively high proportion of respondents (forty-seven per cent) claimed to be members of local churches, with as many in Nonconformist or Roman Catholics churches as in the Church of England. The figure of forty-seven per cent church membership is unexceptional in so far as it is remarkably similar to the figure of forty-three per cent of respondents claiming to attend a place of worship reported by Research Services Ltd. in their analysis of their *Community Attitudes Survey.* [8] However, it should be noted that Research Services Ltd. 'allowed even infrequent visitors (such as for marriages, christenings etc.) to be included in our liberal definition of attendance'. [9] The questionnaire used for this study employed the concept of church membership rather than that of simple attendance. It may be, therefore, that the figure of forty-seven per cent church membership among the activists interviewed is further above the national average than might appear from a superficial comparison with the *Community Attitudes Survey* figures.

Whether or not this is the case, some of the activists made comments which specifically related their involvement in a ratepayer movement to their moral commitment to the Christian religion. For example, an active Roman Catholic commented, 'I believe that if you enjoy life, you ought to try and give something back to the community. If you're one of those people, you tend to get involved either because you have a moral conscience or because you feel you ought to'.

Involvement of this kind need not, of course, be directed towards a local ratepayer movement. There are a number of other organisations which offer equally adequate outlets for the individual with feelings of moral responsibility towards the community. One possibility is that the individual may involve himself in a large number of organisations. A number of the activists interviewed did in fact fit into the category of 'habitual activists'. However, although one or two individuals of this type were found in every area studied, they represent a minority of all the activists interviewed. Only twenty-four per cent of those interviewed belonged to four or more local organisations, a figure not greatly in excess of the thirteen per cent of the *Community Attitude Survey's* sample who belonged to four or more organisations. [10] Many of the activists tended to concentrate their energies on their ratepayers' association, and in fact fifteen per cent of those interviewed had previous experience of ratepayer association activity in a former place of residence.

As Dowse and Hughes point out, 'there is not as the pluralist literature seems to suggest an almost mechanical reaction to outrage'. [11] One should not exaggerate the difficulties of encouraging an individual to become active in a ratepayer movement in the first instance. Very often, it is sufficient to ask an individual to join or he joins in an effort to resolve some personal dispute with the local authority:

> I don't know quite (how I came to get involved). It just happened. I'd never been interested in local government affairs before I retired, but I happened to go to the first ratepayers' association meeting. I got up and asked a question and I was a marked man.
> Because of the distress caused by flooding and no action on the part of the Council.

However, 'intervening is a massively time-consuming and laborious activity', [12] particularly if the movement becomes involved in contesting local elections. If individuals are to continue to be active, they have to acquire new motivations which transcend the flattery of being asked or concern with a particular personal grievance. Very often, ratepayer associations became dependent on one or two individuals with considerable energy and organising skills, possibly motivated by the kinds of consideration discussed earlier in the chapter. The loss of one or two key activists, for whatever reasons, can severely damage an association's chances of survival. The advantage that ratepayer associations in retirement areas enjoy because lack of time is less of a problem for their members is offset by the greater risk of losing key members through ill health or death.

It is therefore not surprising that local ratepayer movements are generally ephemeral. As Steed comments, '. . . their main problem is their lack of staying power . . . many of the Ratepayer groups seem to collapse as rapidly as they arise'. [13] Similarly, Lee comments of Cheshire, 'Ratepayers' and Residents' associations were . . . ephemeral and depended for their effectiveness on one or two people who brought them into existence'. [14] In the short run, large numbers of people may be mobilised behind a campaign to tackle a perceived local grievance, but persuading individuals to undertake the tedious work of maintaining an organisation in being in the long run is rather more difficult. Nevertheless, there are some localities where ratepayer movements have survived long enough for them to be described as persistent features of the local political system. In these situations, they begin to exert an influence on the overall character of the system; for example, their continued existence may affect the behaviour of the major political parties.

This chapter, then, recognises that each local political system is a miniature political system in its own right, but it also attempts to explore the ways in which particular local environments set the parameters within which particular kinds of local political system develop. In order to do this, two case studies will be presented: one of a rapidly expanding area with a persistent local party; the other a resort town with a retiree-based ratepayer movement.

The town of Billericay, Essex is situated some twenty-five miles from London on the Liverpool Street to Southend railway line. Originally part of the Basildon Urban District, based on the new town of Basildon to the south, it now forms part of the non-metropolitan Basildon District which covers an area similar to that served by the predecessor authority. Billericay is a predominantly non-manual (fifty-six per cent of the population in 1966) commuter town which has expanded its population substantially over the last twenty-five years; from 7,400 in 1951 to 17,246 in 1961 and 25,972 in 1971. Since 1960 it has had an active and successful Residents' movement which has been represented on the district (and more recently) the county council. [15]

The trigger action which reinvigorated the Residents' movement in Billericay (the main association traced its lineage back to 1927) and led to its intervention in local elections was the development of an industrial estate in the town. A protest meeting organised by the Residents' Association attracted five hundred people. [16] The concerns of the opponents of the industrial estate were summarised in a statement issued at the time by the Billericay Residents' Association which stated: 'The whole point of the campaign is to stress that the site should be carefully and attractively developed and that the type of work made available should be that which would find the largest amount of potential labour and not serve the interests of the minority.' [17] The nature of this 'minority' was made clear in a letter in the same local newspaper issue in which the statement was printed which argued that 'it is wrong for the complete area to be given over to factories when the majority of residents are not artisans'. [18]

Despite a prolonged campaign, the Residents were (not surprisingly) unable to halt the development of the industrial estate. However, apparently encouraged by the success of Residents' Associations in other parts of the country in electing councillors (particularly at nearby Hornchurch), the Residents decided to contest the 1960 urban district council elections. Although they failed by 262 votes to defeat the least successful Conservative incumbent, they were encouraged by what could be regarded as a good result in a previously 'safe' Conservative ward.

During the ensuing year the local press gave a certain amount of unfavourable publicity to 'party wrangling' in the local council chamber which probably helped the Residents to propagate their argument that party politics should be kept out of local government. In general, Basildon Urban District was no exception to the nationwide pattern of Conservative gains in the 1961 local elections. The Labour Party lost three seats to the Conservatives, but these successes were offset in Billericay by the defeat of the retiring Conservative council chairman by the Residents' Association candidate with a comfortable majority of 595 votes.

A new issue emerged in the autumn of 1961, when the Residents opposed a number of separate planning proposals for the erection of blocks of flats in the Billericay area. Two stormy public meetings were held on the subject in January 1962 and in the May 1962 elections the Residents won three seats from the

Conservatives. The least successful Residents' candidate had a majority of over 1,100 votes over her nearest Conservative rival. These victories gave the Residents the balance of power on Basildon Council. In the election for Chairman of the Council, they supported a Conservative nominee. The senior Residents' councillor was elected chairman of the key Finance Committee, although there was no formal coalition.

In the 1963 elections, the Residents gained a further seat on the Council and retained the seat of a councillor who had been elected for one year in 1962. However, their overall share of the poll dropped from fifty-one per cent to thirty-nine per cent. This decline in electoral support was reflected in troubles within the two associations that made up the Residents' movement in Billericay. The main Billericay association adopted a motion that its priorities should be firstly finance and membership, secondly its magazine, and thirdly Council elections. The association serving the Buttsbury area of the town was also in trouble. Only nineteen members attended a meeting in February 1964 at which the main item on the agenda was 'Survival of the association'. One member at the meeting commented, 'When the area was first developed, five or six years ago, the Association had to contend with a vast lack of public services and facilities, but almost all these problems have now been solved and there is very little for the Association to do'. [19] In other words, the 'underlying sustaining factors' created by an expanding area situation were beginning to disappear.

In the 1964 local election, the Residents lost the seat they were defending by twelve votes. In the spring of 1965, a proposal to construct an 'Inner Relief Road' along a line near the town centre aroused considerable local opposition, but it is perhaps significant that this dissent was spearheaded not by the Residents' Associations, but by a so-called 'County Development Plan Action Group' comprising representatives of the Conservative and Liberal parties, the Billericay Residents' Association, the Council for the Preservation of Rural England and the local Business and Professional Association. The three Residents' candidates were decisively defeated in the 1965 local elections, their most successful candidate receiving 757 votes less than the least successful Conservative candidate.

The Residents did not contest the 1966 elections, but the division of the Billericay Ward into three separate wards in 1967 encouraged them to try again. One of their candidates was successful—in the Central Ward, where Council proposals for the re-development of the High Street had met with considerable criticism. The Residents gained an additional seat in a by-election in August 1967, but lost it the following year when none of their candidates was returned, although they polled between thirty-eight and forty-five per cent of the poll in their wards. However, in 1969 they won two of the three vacant seats in the Billericay wards. In May 1970, they won all three vacant seats and gained another two seats in subsequent by-elections, thus increasing their total strength on the council to eight seats.

With the approach of the 1971 elections, it was apparent that the prospects of the parties were such that the Residents might once again hold the balance of power between Conservative and Labour on Basildon Council. The residents denied any intention of forming a coalition with either side after rumours that Labour was going to offer them the chairmanship of the Works Committee. [20] Their spokesman declared, 'Coalition talk is rubbish. We are totally independent and we will judge each issue separately'. [21] The results of the elections did, in fact, give the Residents the balance of power and one of their senior councillors restated the view that whichever group had the majority should be left to get on with the job of shaping the new council. Labour had won more seats than the Conservatives and Residents' abstentions allowed a Labour nominee to be elected Chairman of the Council. They did, however, subsequently support the Conservatives on one crucial issue in the council chamber; a Labour move to stop council house sales was defeated.

When the first elections for the Basildon District Council were held in 1973, the Residents managed to take six of the nine Billericay seats, losing the other three by a small margin. They also entered county politics for the first time, winning one seat on the new Essex County Council. In 1976 they still held six seats on Basildon District Council, sixteen years after they had first entered local politics.

Particularly in the early years of the residents' movement, their candidates for the council tended to contrast rather sharply with those put forward by the Conservatives. The Conservatives tended to favour small businessmen; the residents' candidates tended to be men in intermediate non-manual jobs who commuted daily to London. Whereas forty-three per cent of Conservative council candidates in Billericay over the decade 1960–1970 came from the Registrar-General's Social Class 1, only sixteen per cent of the Resident's candidates were in this category, but forty per cent were in Social Class 3. Fifteen (fifty-four per cent) of the Conservative candidates for which data was available were local businessmen. In the early 1960's the Residents were often publicly critical of what they saw as the dominant position of small businessmen among local Conservative candidates. For example, an editorial in the magazine of the Billericay Residents' Association commented in 1963: '(The local Conservative chairman) asks us to believe that when his committee put up the butcher, the baker and the candlestick maker, that they acquire a magical ability which enables them to look after our interests better than anyone else.' [22]

The popular image of a ratepayers' association is a body firmly located at the 'save' end of the 'save-spend' dimension in local politics. Many associations of this type do exist, but it is difficult to fit the Residents' movement in Billericay into this category. The election manifestos of the movement have not generally laid any excessive stress on the question of the rates or the rating system. The Billericay association has not been slow to accuse the local Council of a 'pinch-penny attitude' [23] on the provision of facilities and a ten-point policy programme submitted to a meeting in October 1969 made no mention of the rates.

Two complementary themes have been stressed by the Residents' movement in Billericay. On the one hand, there has been a stress on the need to retain at least some semblance of the present nature and character of Billericay' [24] and to prevent the town from becoming 'another "suburbia", a sprawling mass of homes without a heart and soul'. [25] It has also been pointed out that 'The rapid provision of new houses in large numbers has given many families the chance to enjoy urban life in pleasant and healthy surroundings but without the modern urban facilities which many people automatically expect'. [26] Further expansion of the town on a large scale has been argued to be undesirable both because it would destroy its character and further overload overstrained services such as schools and rail services. Thus, expansion helped to generate what was, in many ways, an anti-expansionist movement.

The programme of the Residents' movement in Billericay bears a remarkable similarity to the 'community conservationist' ideology outlined by Agger, Goldrich and Swanson on the basis of their studies of American community politics. The 'community conservationist' ideology seems to have developed in a community ('Oretown') very similar to Billericay in the 1960's: 'The increased population created problems. The influx of people complicated service and housekeeping functions of local government. An expanded school system was necessary to accommodate the children of the young, newcomer families. Basic services had to be expanded to rapidly developed areas of the town . . . There was increased concern for the future of property values and aesthetic standards'. [27]

Agger et al. distinguish a number of elements in the 'community conservationist' ideology. Community conservationists 'view the community as a complex of mutually interdependent parts in which the individual good and the common good are naturally compatible, if not identical. They see the values of community life maximised when political leadership is exercised by men representing the public at large, rather than "special interests" '. [28] The theme of a readily discernible common good is apparent in statements made by the Billericay Residents' movement. For example, the Residents have expressed the view that the loyalties of national party councillors are 'torn between their political party and the local needs of Billericay'. [29] Party politics leads to 'the needs of the town' being disregarded. Among the campaign slogans the movement has used are 'A vote for X is a vote for your local interests' and 'Put Billericay first'. Of course, from time to time the associations have to take a position on issues which divide the national political parties. Reference has already been made to the movement's support for the sale of council houses. Apart from housing, comprehensive education has been one of the most controversial issues in British local politics. In 1970, when the Conservative Leader of the Council proposed the establishment of two new grammar schools in the Urban District, the Buttsbury Residents' Association criticised the proposal as 'impractical and disruptive' and declared its support for the existing system of comprehensive secondary education. [30]

A further element of community conservationism is a stress on the need for 'long-range planning in the public interest . . . There is a socialist-like emphasis on community planning without the socialist objective of increased public ownership of the means of production.' [31] The first election manifesto of the Residents' movement, issued in 1960, placed a greater emphasis on the need for 'good' planning than any other issue. In 1970 a Residents' candidate in a by-election stated, 'In Billericay, planning in my opinion is the number one issue. So much planning today looks only two or three years ahead, which is wrong. Planning should be very forward thinking, and should look ten to fifteen years ahead.' [32]

The community conservationists studied by Agger and his colleagues 'were not low tax people; nor did they seem very much concerned with who paid how much, as long as needed programs . . . were provided'. [33] The Residents' movement in Billericay may be fitted into this mould; their emphasis has been rather on the provision of adequate facilities out of public funds rather than on the pursuit of economy as a dominant priority.

The rise of a new political movement like a Residents' Association may affect the operation of a local political system in a number of ways. It may affect the activity patterns of other political groups in the area, the content of decisions, and the modes of behaviour and decision-taking within the local council.

The emergence of the Residents' movement in Billericay seems to have been perceived as a particularly threatening occurrence by the existing political parties. It may be that this type of reaction is common to all situations involving the emergence of a new political movement. [34] New political movements introduce uncertainty into stable political situations, and this uncertainty increases the costs of operation of established political movements, even if these movements are not frustrated in any way in the achievement of their goals. More specifically, these costs may be categorised as follows:

1. Organisational. If a 'symbolic' electoral contest is replaced by a 'real' electoral contest, as happened in Billericay, more effort may have to be expended on such activities as canvassing. Workers may have to be deployed into the formerly 'safe' area, thus weakening the deploying party's competitive position in 'traditional' marginal seats.

2. 'Ideological'. 'The world as we know it' of party activists is threatened. Activists are conditioned to responding to the arguments of existing parties. New parties may introduce a new political dimension which necessitates re-thinking and existing ideologies may be exposed as inadequate. The existing party can, of course, choose as a tactic whether or not to argue with the new party on the latter's terms. Thus, there was a debate within the Scottish Labour Party at the time of the rise of Scottish Nationalism in the late 1960's about whether the party should discuss contemporary questions in terms of what would happen in an independent Scottish state, or whether they should ignore the existence of the Nationalists completely. Whilst an established party can choose to ignore an insurgent party, it may not be able politically to afford to do so, and the intra-party debate about how to react may itself be highly disruptive.

The overall effect of these imposed costs is to impair the ability of the established party to function effectively. In the early days of the emergence of the Residents' movement in Billericay, the then Chairman of the local Conservative Association issued a statement containing the following passage: 'The really worrying thing is that we may see in Billericay such a spread of "R.A.ism" that the Conservative Association gets seriously weakened and submerged by the R.A. movement . . . The entry of the R.A. into local politics looks harmless enough at the moment, while there is an adequate Conservative majority locally, and no General Election in prospect nationally. But while wishing a "non-electoral" R.A. well, I think that they —and all anti-Socialists who support them at elections—are now playing with fire in a bigger context. I would ask you to continue to support the Conservative Association in order that the way is not left open for Labour to overtake us, locally and nationally, while we squabble and play with words, and so weaken our ability to resist.' [35]

The persistence of 'R.A.ism' in Billericay seems to have had a somewhat debilitating effect on the morale of the local Conservatives. In 1971 there was no official Conservative candidate in one of the Billericay wards. It was reported that a considerable number of people had been approached but all had refused nomination. The Conservative branch chairman commented, 'Nobody wants to be a loser.' [36] After the 1971 elections, the sole remaining Conservative councillor announced his intention not to stand again, telling his branch to 'find another mug'. [37] In the event, he did stand the next year because the party was once again short of candidates.

The local Liberals were also unhappy about the rise of the Residents' movement in Billericay, possibly because they felt that the strength of the Residents' Association was preventing Billericay from being turned into the 'Orpington of Essex'. The local Liberal leader stated, 'There can be very savage results from minorities like the Residents who reject everything. Groups similar to the Residents' Association gave rise to Fascism. They are a cancerous growth on the face of the community'. [38] A local Labour leader also subsequently alleged that the Residents were creating conditions in which 'Fascist thugs would be able to take over'. [39]

The influence of the Residents on the council may have been reduced by their insistence that they were not a political party. Their councillors have not been 'whipped', although this situation has not prevented them from voting together on major issues. When they were interviewed by the local newspaper on the town's 'three most controversial topics' [40] after the 1971 elections, their replies revealed a remarkable degree of unanimity.

Nevertheless, the Residents' insistence on the 'independence' of their councillors has created problems from time to time. The absence of formal links between the Residents' Association and the councillors did create some difficulties, especially in the early years. At one stage a leading Ratepayer councillor was invited to come to Billericay from Hornchurch to deliver an appropriate 'ex cathedra' doctrinal pronouncement. This he did, drawing a distinction between the 'independence of arrogance' and the 'independence of conscience'.

The Residents' insistence that they were not a political party also made it difficult on occasions for their representatives to accommodate themselves to some of the Council's routine arrangements for the regulation of business. Standing Order Number 5 of Basildon Urban District Council stated: 'Any political party represented on the Council may appoint a Leader and Deputy Leader of such party from time to time and on notification of the name of such persons in writing to the

Clerk such persons shall be so recognised by the Council'.

Following an enquiry from the Town Manager, the Residents reiterated their position that 'that Residents Associations' councillors do not consider themselves to be members of a Political Party (and are) therefore unable to elect a Leader and Deputy Leader within the terms of the Council's Standing Order No.5'. [41] However, clearly the Residents' leaders appreciated that if they did not make some arrangements to fit in with the Council's conventions, their opportunities for influence might be diminished. They therefore appointed a 'formal representative' and a 'deputy to the formal representative'. In this way, they were able to preserve the form of not being a political party, whilst at the same time conforming to the arrangements necessary for the smooth running of the Council's business.

As has been pointed out, the Residents have held the balance of power between Conservative and Labour on Basildon Council on two occasions. Although the Residents have sometimes had a crucial impact on the decisions on the Council (for example, on the sale of council houses), they have had relatively little success with their own major crusades, e.g. their early crusade on the industrial estate or their later crusade on the Inner Relief Road which the Council endorsed in 1971 (although two Conservatives and six Labour councillors broke ranks to support the Residents on this issue). Very often the decisions the Residents have been fighting are really taken at a higher level. Their belated entry into county politics shows that they have partially recognised this fact. However, the fact remains that what 'localist' parties of this type want is often contrary to national policy, and, of course, they are generally unable to exert leverage at the national level. This problem is the fundamental limitation of the 'purely local party; success at the local level is often not enough to attain their goals'.

The Residents' movement in Billericay is one of the few movements of this type which has been able to entrench itself as part of a local political system (another example is in Havering in Greater London). Its persistence cannot be explained simply in terms of the continuing growth of Billericay (the rate of expansion has slowed down in recent years) or of specific local issues.

In many ways, the first few years are most crucial for a ratepayer movement. If it can survive the early years, its chances of remaining in being as a successful movement are high. First, its councillors and activists develop a considerable commitment to the organisation. One of the Residents councillors in Billericay has been active for nearly fifteen years; another two have been active for ten years. As Stanyer points out, 'A firm distinction must be drawn ... between the individuals who are first considering entering local politics and those who have been councillors for some time'. [42] Those councillors who are long-serving members of a council may develop all kinds of attachment to the council and its work that lead them to devote a considerable proportion of their energies to seeking re-election. In the case of the Residents councillors, this includes ensuring that the Residents' Association remains a lively and active body. Secondly, a Residents' movement that is electorally successful in the long run becomes an established channel of recruitment that attracts new activists who are eager to become councillors.

76

Thirdly, as the movement's leadership acquires experience, they become more politically sophisticated. They are no longer 'political outsiders' using inappropriate tactics to secure their ends: [43] they are often able to beat the established parties at their own game. In the case of Billericay, the Residents' movement seems to have enjoyed a young, well educated, relatively sophisticated leadership from the beginning. They did not raise the expectations of their followers to an excessively high level. Many ratepayer movements, particularly the 'fanatical economisers', exaggerate (often because of their lack of political knowledge) the difference their presence on the council will make. They quickly find that dropping a twinning scheme or not giving the mayor a new car will not produce large savings and that considerable savings can only be made by cutting services in a way that might be unacceptable to large sections of the electorate or by cutting staff in a way that might be unacceptable to the local government unions.

The Billericay Residents have never been obsessive economisers; rather they have concentrated on an ethic of 'community service'. In a sence, they were pioneers of the 'community politics' that was much in vogue at the beginning of the 1970's; they concentrated on taking action on relatively small issues which nevertheless concerned voters and on keeping a relatively well educated electorate informed about the council's business through the medium of two well produced journals. Indeed, the Buttsbury association in particular achieved a ratio of members to voters that most local branches of the national political parties would envy. [44] The following quotations from a small-scale sample survey carried out by the author in Billericay give some indication of the electorate's response to this strategy: 'The Residents, they're very keen, they let us know what is happening, which I think is a very good thing' (Motor fitter, 32); 'They do voice the opinions of the people, they try to listen to what people want' (Postman's wife, 53); 'Locally, the Residents seem to be pretty good, they seem to work for the local community as they're not part of larger party politics' (Student, 19).

The Residents' movement developed in Billericay in a community which had a number of problems arising from rapid expansion. The consolidation of the Residents' position may in part be attributed to the recognition of their leadership that there was a demand for a particular style of community politics which eschewed national political issues and concentrated on relatively trivial issues which were nevertheless of concern to the electorate. The socio-economic environment of Billericay created favourable conditions for the development of a Residents' movement, but the skill of the movement's leadership (admittedly readily available in a middle class commuter town) helped to sustain the movement in being once the initial grievances had been resolved.

Seaton, Devon

The Urban District of Seaton, situated on the south coast of Devon, had a population of 4,140 in 1971; forty-two per cent of the population were of pensionable age (compared with twenty-eight per cent in 1951 and thirty-three per cent in 1961). A Ratepayers' Association had been active in Seaton in the 1950's, at one time having four representatives on the local council, and in 1963 thirty people attended a meeting organised in an effort to revive the Association . . . The meeting was told that 'there was a great need for a ratepayers' association in Seaton . . . with so many matters vitally affecting householders under consideration'. The question of rating assessments, the threatened closure of the local railway line, and the regrouping of water undertakings were referred to as specific examples. [45]

By November 1963 the reconstitued Association had 250 members. The first traceable reference to any conflict of interest between Seaton traders and the Ratepayers' Association is in a press report of a discussion on the future of the town at the annual general meeting in May 1964. Some of the speakers pointed out that people coming to Seaton to retire did so in search of peace and quiet, but traders naturally wanted to attract as many people as possible during the holiday season. The possibility of there being a conflict of interest between the two groups was posed as question rather than as a statement of fact, and it was agreed to seek a meeting with the traders to see if a break could be avoided and a common policy agreed. [46]

This initiative was evidently unsuccessful, for in 1965 the Ratepayers contested the Urban District Council elections and defeated two (independent) candidates seeking re-election. One of the defeated candidates spoke critically of the membership of the Ratepayers' Association as consisting 'largely of elderly and retired people, most of whom have come only recently to live in the district'. [47] A Ratepayers' Association spokesman denied that the Association's membership consisted largely of old people, but went on to argue, 'The town depends to a great extent on retired people for its livelihood. They are mostly of the executive class with pensions additional to the state pension . . . They intend to take every practical step to keep Seaton an attractive resort wherein they can, for most of the year, enjoy its lovely position'. [48] This exchange marks the start of a conflict between the Ratepayers' Association and some commercial interests in the town which reached a high pitch in the winter of 1969/70.

In November 1966, a retiree who subsequently became a leader of the Ratepayers' Association published an open letter to the Urban District Council entitled 'Which way Seaton?'. This document is worth quoting at length because it illustrates some of the central concerns of the retirees: 'My wife and I were very concerned at the apparent intention of the Council, in collaboration with the Chamber of Trade, to look around and see what further amenities can be provided to attract holidaymakers to Seaton.' After stating that many holidaymakers come to Seaton because of its 'Natural charm . . . smallness (and) quietness', the writer of the letter went on to outline in some detail the contribution he considered that retirees make to the local economy. The letter concluded, 'In my opinion Seaton is at the parting of the ways. Is it to go forward, be progressive and be developed into a funfair—a Blackpool of the South—or is it to be preserved for those people, holidaymakers and residents alike, who value its natural charm?' [49]

It is this type of question—and particularly the phrase 'Blackpool of the South'—which recurs time and time again in exchanges between the Ratepayers and their opponents. It was not, however, until the summer of 1969 that the Ratepayers' Association as a body took any firm, public position on the question 'What kind of town shall ours be?' The question had been aired on several occasions at its meetings, but, whilst there was little doubt about the direction of its sympathies, it had not committed itself to any open condemnation of existing policies.

However, in the early summer of 1969, the Ratepayers' Association published an article in its newsletter which formed the basis of a subsequent report in the local newspaper which stated: 'Criticism of Seaton's efforts to attract holidaymakers have been voiced in no uncertain terms by various members of the local Ratepayers' Association, who claim that the tone of the town is being lowered in the process. Facts and figures quoted in the Association's current newsletter are said to show that the residents provide the bulk of the town's revenue, while tourism benefits only the traders.'

The newsletter article itself started: 'The "policy" . . . is to fill the town in the season to overflowing, to allow holiday flats, chalets and camps to multiply, ostensibly to meet a need but calculated to create a demand . . . The only section of our community which stands to gain from this is a small, but articulate, part of the trading element. Residential property owners will lose heavily. The above would be unbearable even if the commercial section were paying for it; but they are not.' [50]

The Chamber of Trade's immediate reaction was that 'if the business community is prospering, then the town as a whole will benefit'. Later in the year, the Chamber felt constrained to ask whether the Urban District Council was taking tourism seriously enough, 'considering it was the town's bread and butter'. [51] The response of the Ratepayers' Association was to issue a statement arguing that the economy of Seaton should be based 'fairly and squarely' upon its development as a residential seaside town. No further amenities should be provided out of the rates purely to attract visitors, and existing camp sites should either be modernised or discontinued. Holidaymakers who liked a clean and unspoilt place would continue to come to Seaton; those who wanted another kind of holiday would go elsewhere. Therefore, the quality of visitors would improve. The Chamber of Trade's proposals for the future of the town were criticised as being based 'on an expansionist policy first and foremost for the benefit of the commercial interests in Seaton'. [52]

This statement provoked a number of letters to the local paper which appeared under the heading 'Seaton—a town for the elderly or popular holiday resort?' in its next issue. One letter writer declared, 'What the burgesses must decide for themselves is, do they want the town to be run by a minority group of elderly people who have no interest in the prosperity of the inhabitants at large, or do they want Seaton to progress as a leading holiday resort in Devon?' [53] Another letter writer argued, 'There are those, with sincere desires to see what they regard as progress, who would like, for fourteen glorious weeks, to have the candy floss, funfairs, coloured lights and carnivals. The question is, who pays? And who, after the visitors have gone, picks up the letter and repairs the damage? Seaton has got to decide what it wants to be—Blackpool or Bournemouth. It can't be both.' [54]

In what appeared to be an attempt to reduce the level of conflict, the Chairman of the Urban District Council criticised the policies of both the Ratepayers' Association and the Chamber of Trade. However, this attempt at honest brokerage seems to have had little perceptible effect. The Chamber of Trade demanded that the town's expansion programme should be implemented immediately. [56] The Ratepayers' Association sought, and obtained, the endorsement of its members for its policy of developing Seaton as a natural resort. [56]

Although conflict did subside to some extent, the Ratepayers' Association continued to be active in local politics. Local government reorganisation brought about the incorporation of the Seaton Urban District in the new East Devon District. The Ratepayers were successful in electing one member to the new authority. However, when he retired in 1976, he was not replaced.

Thirteen of the fourteen members of the executive committee of Seaton Ratepayers' Association were interviewed in the summer of 1970. All the thirteen activists interviewed were retired persons who had formerly followed non-manual occupations and had moved to Seaton to retire. The mean age of the committee was sixty-eight years and their mean length of residents in the town 6.6 years

When asked what they considered to be the main tasks of a ratepayers' association, nine of the thirteen respondents gave answers centring on the restriction of the level of Council spending. A number of the activists put forward the view that the particular situation of retired people in resort towns fostered the development of what they termed 'rates consciousness'. For example: '(One has) more time to think about it. People come to seaside resorts because we wanted to come and find that rates are rather higher compared with what we left, and you become more rates conscious.'

Only two respondents placed a primary emphasis in their answers on the preservation of the area. However, it was clear from the replies to other questions that 'preservation' was an issue of central concern for the activists. In particular, they were anxious to prevent Seaton from being turned into a 'second Blackpool': 'A lot of people want this town to get like a second Blackpool. We don't want it. Ratepayers want to keep it as we found it.'

None of the respondents wanted to discourage visitors altogether. There was, however, a feeling that Seaton was attracting the wrong type of visitor and that this trend would continue if policy was not reversed:

> There's a certain amount of spoilation of the town by an excess of the type of visitor of the caravanning and tenting variety mainly who leave their litter about and generally spoil the niceness of the town for residents in the holiday months.

The basic objectives of the Ratepayers' Association was summarised by a resondent who stated:

I think that the Ratepayers' Association's aims are what I want and what I approve of, to keep it as a good residential district, to attract a good class of visitor, but not necessarily to overcrowd it or produce funfairs.

These two themes complement one another in so far as opposition to the 'vulgarisation' of the resort by the provision of additional 'attractions' out of municipal revenues is consistent with a desire to limit council spending. The leadership of the Ratepayers' Association generally held to the view that conflict with 'the commercial element' in the town was inevitable. It was felt that 'the benefit of the tourist trade goes almost entirely into private hands. The ratepayers finance many kinds of extra expenditure, but get nothing in return'. This led the Ratepayers leaders to perceive the town as being split into two sections:

Part of the Council are representative of the trade and commerce of Seaton and the other part is representative of the 'new Seatonians'.

One of the leaders of the Ratepayers' Association did, however, subdivide the 'trade and commerce' of Seaton into two distinct components. As he saw it, the shopkeepers were all-the-year round traders and were therefore much more reliant on residents' custom than the hoteliers. This led the shopkeepers to adopt a less intransigent political position than the hoteliers. These qualifications aside, he considered that: 'In all seaside resorts, you are bound to have a certain conflict of interests between the commercial element and the private residential element . . . The R.A. is representing the private element . . . I think you will find that pretty well all seaside towns have a R.A., you have these two conflicting elements'.

The Ratepayers' Association did not, in fact, aim to gain control of the Urban District Council but only to obtain a 'balance of power' with the traders. The Association was prepared to endorse candidates it did not initially sponsor, but who subsequently attracted its favour by their actions in the council chamber. Thus, just prior to each council election, every one of the Association's nine hundred members received a note on recommended candidates. The note reproduced below was issued immediately before the 1970 Urban District Council elections:

We understand that Councillors A and B will be standing for re-election and Mrs. C. who is a member of the Executive Committee will be standing as a new candidate. These three will have the official support of the Association. We also understand that Councillor D will stand for re-election. Although in the past Mr. D has not relied on the backing of this Association, he is in fact a member and in view of his good work as a Councillor he is worthy of our support.

The only candidate to be unsuccessful in this particular election was a shopkeeper who had not received the endorsement of the Ratepayers' Association.

Seaton as an urban district presented a classic example of the type of resort conflict situation discussed in the analytical framework presented in the last chapter. The Ratepayers' movement in the town was led by a committee of retired newcomers from non-manual occupational backgrounds, its membership was largely made up of similar people, and it safeguarded their interests with the aid of a carefully thought out programme which emphasised the special contribution of the retiree of the economy and general well-being of the town. Its policy of 'preserving' the town and curtailing rates expenditure on tourist attractions was opposed by an equally articulate group of traders and conflict between these two groups inevitably resulted.

Three other Devon seaside towns—Sidmouth, Exmouth and Dawlish—were studied as part of the research. All three had experienced active Ratepayer movements. In Sidmouth the Ratepayers were involved in a controversy over a proposal to build a golf course in the town in an attempt to turn it into 'the St. Andrews of the west'. This scheme was backed by local hoteliers, but the Ratepayers' Association regarded it as an expensive white elephant. They organised a referendum on the scheme, and a vote of 3,102 to 140 against was recorded, but the Council decided to proceed with the construction of the course by the Chairman's casting vote. The Ratepayers' Association contested the next local elections and unseated four councillors. Subsequently, relations between the Council and the Ratepayers' Association improved. No doubt councillors felt that they had to take notice of an Association with over 2,000 members; moreover, the Council's strategy of developing Sidmouth as a 'select resort' seemed to meet with the general approval of retired people in the town.

Exmouth also had a long history of Ratepayer activity, which reached its peak in 1963 when a Ratepayer/Tenant alliance won five of the seven vacant Urban District Council Seats. This alliance of a ratepayers' association 'opposed to unnecessary spending of large sums of public money' and concerned 'about retired folk who cannot stretch their pensions any more' with a movement of council tenants is somewhat unusual. However, according to the then Chairman of the Ratepayers' Association what he described as the Ratepayer/Tenant 'solid front' was necessary because 'there was not real conflict between the Conservative and Labour members (on Exmouth Council). They were united in the council chamber, and in such a battle the 'Independents' must fight as one'. [57]

In Dawlish the Ratepayers' Association was revitalised to fight an expensive sewerage scheme on the grounds that 'the camp proprietors would benefit far more than the ordinary residents'. The Association was very much concerned with the plight of the 'third of Dawlish ratepayers (who are) retired people on fixed incomes'. By 1964, the Ratepayers' Association had elected eight representatives to the local Urban District Council. However, 'internal wrangles began to crop up within the Association and the initial enthusiasm of the ordinary members soon turned into disillusionment'. [58] In addition, the Association had aroused expectations to an excessively high level: 'Some bold statements were made about reducing the rates if the association could sponsor enough councillors. But they failed to work any miracles and the rates kept on rising.' [59]

In this chapter an attempt has been made to illustrate how particular kinds of local political environment can foster the development of ratepayer and resident movements. The case studies of Billericay and Seaton show that rapidly expanding towns and resort communities with large retired populations can develop patterns of conflict which result in the formation and survival of 'genuine local parties'. Nevertheless, it is not implied that this kind of response to a particular set of local political circumstances is an automatic one. The way in which the conflicts present in such communities develop will depend to a considerable extent on the decisions made by those individuals who choose to become involved in local politics. In particular, it is clear that the ephemerality or otherwise of a ratepayers' or residents' movement can depend to a considerable extent on the skill and energies of a few key activists.

Notes

[1] M. Olson Jnr, *The Logic of Collective Action,* Shocken Books, New York 1968, p.2.
[2] Ibid., pp.15—16.
[3] R.E. Dowse and J. Hughes, 'Sporadic Interventionists', *Political Studies,* vol.25, no.1, March 1977, pp.84—92, p.90.
[4] J.Q. Wilson, *The Amateur Democrat,* University of Chicago Press, Chicago 1963, p.226.
[5] Ibid., p.226.
[6] Ibid., p.223.
[7] R.T. Holt and J.E. Turner, *Political Parties in Action,* Collier-Macmillan, London 1968, p.253.
[8] Royal Commission on Local Government in England, Research Studies 9, *Community Attitudes Survey:* England, HMSO, London 1969, p.51.
[9] Ibid., p.60.
[10] Ibid., p.53.
[11] Dowse and Hughes, op.cit., p.90.
[12] Ibid., p.90.
[13] M. Steed, 'Ratepayers Associations and Local Politics' (Part 2), *Insight,* July 1965, pp.14—21, p.21.
[14] J.M. Lee, *Social Leaders and Public Persons,* Clarendon Press, Oxford 1963, p.203.
[15] A number of activists in Billericay were interviewed as part of the original research, but because of an undertaking given at the time no use has been made of the interview material.
[16] *The Times,* 6 October 1959.
[17] Statement issued by Billericay Residents' Association.
[18] *Billericay Times,* 5 October 1959.
[19] *Brentwood Gazette,* 15 February 1964.
[20] *Billericay Standard-Recorder,* 7 May 1971.
[21] *Billericay Standard-Recorder,* 21 May 1971.

[22] *Billericay Observer,* 26 September 1961.

[23] *Mayflower* (journal of the Billericay Residents' Association), No.9.

[24] *Buttsbury News* (journal of the Buttsbury Residents' Association), January 1971.

[25] Statement submitted by Buttsbury Residents' Association to town planning inquiry, 26 April 1970.

[26] By-election bulletin of Buttsbury Residents' Association, November 1970.

[27] R.E. Agger, D. Goldrich, B.E. Swanson, *The Rulers and the Ruled,* Wiley, New York 1964, p.136.

[28] Ibid., p.21.

[29] *Buttsbury News,* May 1970.

[30] *Buttsbury News,* September 1970.

[31] Agger et al., op.cit., p.25.

[32] *Billericay Standard-Recorder,* 6 November 1970.

[33] Agger et al., op.cit., p.362.

[34] For example, research carried out by the author in two Scottish new towns in 1969 showed that the leaders of the existing political parties felt that they had more in common with each other than with the Scottish Nationalists.

[35] Statement issued in August 1961.

[36] *Billericay Standard-Recorder,* 23 April 1971.

[37] *Billericay Standard-Recorder,* 11 June 1971.

[38] *Billericay Observer,* 3 July 1962.

[39] *Brentwood Gazette,* 21 March 1963.

[40] *Billericay Standard-Recorder,* 21 April 1971.

[41] *Buttsbury News,* September 1970.

[42] J. Stanyer, *Understanding Local Government,* Fontana, London 1976, p.113.

[43] Brier and Dowse draw attention to the use of inappropriate tactics by 'political outsiders'. A.P. Brier and R.E. Dowse, 'Political Mobilisation: a Case Study', *International Review of Community Development,* no.19–20, 1968, pp.327–340, pp.336–7.

[44] For example, in 1971 it had a membership of 1,220 out of a voting strength of 1,570.

[45] *Express and Echo,* Exeter, 19 November 1963.

[46] *Express and Echo,* 1 May 1964.

[47] *Pulman's Weekly News,* 4 June 1965.

[48] Ibid., 4 June 1965.

[49] *Pulman's Weekly News,* 25 January 1966.

[50] From press cuttings supplied by local informant. No precise date given.

[51] Ibid.

[52] *Pulman's Weekly News,* 30 December 1969.

[53] Ibid., 6 January 1970.

[54] Ibid., 6 January 1970.

[55] Ibid., 3 March 1970.

[56] Ibid., 24 March 1970.

[57] *Express and Echo,* 12 May 1964.
[58] Ibid., 23 May 1968.
[59] Ibid., 23 May 1968.

4 Ratepayers in revolt

In local government circles, 1974 is remembered as the year of the ratepayers' revolt. As the then Secretary of State for the Environment, Mr A. Crosland commented' 'Dissatisfaction with the present rating system is now, for understandable reasons, both more violent and more universal than I have known it in my lifetime.' [1] What were the 'understandable reasons'? In this chapter an analytical framework is developed in an attempt to explain the 'new wave' of ratepayer protest movements which has emerged since 1974.

In April 1974 domestic ratepayers in England and Wales started to receive the first demands for payment from the new local authorities created by the reorganisation of local government embodied in the 1972 Local Government Act. As the Layfield Report on Local Government Finance notes: 'The demand notes contained one very clear message for many ratepayers–an unprecedented increase in the total bill compared with previous years. Where in previous years there had been an average increase of around ten per cent, in 1974/5 there was an increase about three times as large for England and Wales as a whole, and for some areas increases excluded one hundred per cent.' [2] In fact, twenty of the twenty-five authorities experiencing increases of over one hundred per cent were in the Yorks and Humberside regions.

Starting with reports of rate rebellions in Northamptonshire and Solihull in April, 'an angry and extensive outburst of protest at the rate increase' [3] developed in England and Wales in the Spring of 1974. In particular, a large number of new ratepayer groups were formed and older groups took on a new lease of life. These developments culminated in the formation in June of a National Association of Ratepayer Action Groups. The National Union of Ratepayer Associations had, of course, existed for many years and at 'successive national conferences sent telegrams to successive Chancellors urging drastic reform of local government finance'. [4] The National Association of Ratepayer Action Groups (NARAG) denounced the National Union of Ratepayer Associations (NURA) as a 'fuddy duddy' [5] organisation and, indeed, NARAG did seem to cultivate a more militant image, although its General Secretary was subsequently to complain about the 'initial burst of national publicity' that had 'too often represented NARAG as a bunch of wild men refusing to pay rates at all and mobilising in millions for marches on town halls'. [6]

Certainly, NARAG bore all the marks of an 'outsider' interest group, that is to say a group that was not politically sophisticated or experienced and therefore had difficulty in making the kind of sustained impact on policy-making that a conventional interest group would hope to achieve. The chairman of one of the most successful of the new ratepayers' associations commented, 'we have attracted those ratepayers who formerly took little interest in politics'. [7] If one looks at the evidence submitted by NARAG to the Layfield Committee, it is apparent that it was compiled by people with little experience of submitting papers to official committees. The results of a survey are calculated to three decimal places, the evidence includes statements such as 'It is not particularly relevant, but we have received comment from Zurich and California, USA', [8] and the statement concludes by making the constitutionally impossible demand that once a new system of local government finance had been introduced, it could only be changed by a 'free and open vote'. [9] in Parliament.

Nevertheless, although it may have been politically unsophisticated, NARAG was certainly not ineffective. Both major political parties moved quickly to defuse the rates row and curb what they undoubtedly saw as the alarming growth of the ratepayer movement. In June, during a debate in the House of Commons on the rating system in which the Government was defeated by nine votes, Mr Crosland announced a full scale inquiry on local government finance subsequently carried out by the Layfield Committee. In July 1974 the Government introduced a special domestic relief to mitigate the effects on domestic ratepayers of the very large rate increases experienced in many areas. On the Conservative side, Mrs. Thatcher (then Conservative environment spokesperson) had met NARAG and in their October manifesto the Conservatives promised to reform the rating system when they returned to power.

In October the Government took steps to prevent a repetition of the 1974 rate rises in 1975. The rate support grant was increased by seventy per cent with the object of restricting average rate increases in 1975 to twenty five per cent; on the whole (with certain exceptions) this objective was achieved. *The Economist* commented: 'So generous has the Secretary of State for the Environment been to the local authorities that the National Association of Ratepayer Action Groups has almost been done out of a job'. [10] NARAG continued to be active, however; by January 1975 it claimed 15,000 members. On the whole, it seemed to be stronger in the North and Midlands, whereas NURA retained its old strength along the southern 'Costa Geriatrica'. However, the mass meetings and extensive publicity of 1974 had disappeared by 1975. This appears to have led to some debate within NARAG about its role. As its 1975 annual general meeting NARAG announced plans to launch the largest non-political (sic) party in Britain. It was decided to seek mergers with other bodies including small businessmen and campaigners for the self-employed. However, this attempt to fan the embers of the middle class revolt seems to have met with little success, although NARAG continues to comment on developments in local government finance.

There can be little doubt that the fear of a new ratepayers revolt was very much in the minds of those concerned with local government in 1975 and 1976, although by 1976 the demands of Britain's international creditors were having a greater impact on local government finance than any revolt of ratepayers. Nevertheless, ratepayer movements possess two formidable sanctions. First, they can contest elections and return their own candidates. Unfortunately for the Ratepayer movement, there were no general local government elections in 1974. Although they scored some substantial successes in the metropolitan districts in 1975 and made more gains in 1976, they did not make the sweeping gains they might have made if elections had been held in 1974. Nevertheless, the fear of being defeated may exert a powerful influence on the minds of councillors; in a marginal ward, a ratepayer candidate only has to secure a few hundred votes to affect the balance between the major parties. Second, they can promote strikes of ratepayers. This is probably a more formidable sanction. Although councils can eventually obtain distress warrants against defaulting ratepayers, it is costly and difficult to act against thousands of ratepayers acting in concert. In fact, local authorities have found ratepayers increasingly resistant to paying their rate demands; for example, in 1975 Croydon had to summon 7,000 ratepayers on distress warrants and Hillingdon 6,410 (about thirteen per cent of all ratepayers). The impact of the ratepayers revolt of 1974 cannot simply be measured in terms of the number of seats they were able to win on councils; much more important was the impact they had on serving councillors, concerned about losing their seats and worried about their council's ability to extract the necessary funds from ratepayers.

It was suggested in Chapter Two that a new analytical framework would be needed to account for the growth of ratepayer movements since local government reorganisation. The framework developed here differs in a fundamental way from that used to account for the differential incidence of ratepayer and similar parties before reorganisation. Whereas the analytical framework developed in Chapter Two saw ratepayer and similar movements largely as a local response to particular sets of local conditions, the analytical framework developed here places much more emphasis on *underlying sustaining factors* which can be found in all local authority areas, although local conditions are also important. In other words, ratepayer movements are not a manifestation of 'localism' to the extent that they used to be.

The analytical framework contains four main propositions. First, it is argued that in all areas there is a hostility to party politics in local government which can be mobilised by ratepayer movements. Second, there is a hostility towards the rating system which can also be mobilised by ratepayer movements. Third, it is argued that such movements are particularly likely to develop where the Conservative party is weak. Fourth, it is argued that the development of such movements is stimulated by exceptionally high rate increases and that they have a tendency to be ephemeral.

Opposition to party politics in local government is, of course, not necessarily confined either to ratepayer movements or, for that matter, to the United Kingdom. The Committee on the Management of Local Government noted in its report that 'The evidence contains much general criticism of the influence of party politics in local government'. [11] The undesirability of party politics in local government was a popular theme among ratepayer movements submitting evidence to the Royal Commission on Local Government in England. For many of the organisations giving evidence to the Royal Commission, opposition to the 'intrusion' of party politics in local government seemed to be very much an article of faith requiring no further justification—only remedial action. For example, Farnham Ratepayers' Association state in their evidence, 'That party politics having no sensible place in local government, there should be no canvassing for election to a local authority by reference to a political party'. [12]

Similar themes emerge from popular debate on local politics in other western countries. In a comment on the 'no party politics' of suburban government in the United States, Wood notes: 'There is . . . an outright reaction against partisan activity, a refusal to recognise that there may be persistent cleavages in the electorate and an ethical disapproval of permanent group collaboration as an appropriate means of settling group disputes'. [13] Similarly, in an assessment of the 'rhetoric of "apolitisme"' in France, Kesselman comments, 'A Socialist deputy mayer unknowingly repeated the classic argument used by the American municipal reform movement to oppose politics when he said, 'For the problem of water, school and roads, there's no Gaullist view and no Communist view. I don't see any reason for the injection of politics. Everyone should agree'. [14]

In an effort to assess the ideological components of the ratepayer movement's rejection of party politics in local government, a list of eight objections to party politics in local government was prepared on the basis of a reading of the literature:

1. The regular stirring up of political feeling in the local community is harmful.
2. Decisions taken on party political grounds discourage officers who see their impartial advice disregarded.
3. Party politics often deter people who would make good councillors from standing for the council.
4. The party group system has a harmful effect on the working local councils by making debates in the council chamber meaningless.
5. Where a ward has a clear majority one way or the other for a particular party, the selection of a councillor is virtually in the hands of the committee of that party.
6. The activities of local authorities are not basically of a party political nature.
7. Local elections are used simply as a means of keeping the party machine in trim and local issues are disregarded.
8. Party politics leads to the adoption of doctrinnaire policies regardless of individual circumstances.

These statements were submitted to thirty-eight ratepayer activists. Respondents were asked whether they disagreed with any of the arguments. The largest number of disagreements (seven) related to the first item 'The regular stirring up of political feeling in the local community is harmful.' Ratepayer movement activists may believe in the absence of party politics, but this does not necessarily mean that they believe in the absence of any form of political conflict. As one respondent put it, 'Quite a lot depends on what the political feeling is about. Sometimes it may be beneficial for it to be stirred up'.

Respondents were asked to arrange in order of preference the three arguments which carried greatest weight with them personally. In preparing the table below, three points were awarded to each first placing; two points were awarded to each second placing; and one point to each third placing. Half points on two items result from a tie for third place given by one respondent.

Table 4.1

Arguments against party politics in local government preferred by ratepayer activists

Ranking on points	Argument (shortened version given)	Total points	First preferences
1	Activities of local authorities not party political	46	11
2	Party group system makes council debate meaningless	40	5
3	Party politics leads to doctrinnaire policies	32	3
4=	Decisions taken on party grounds discourage officers	25	4
4=	Party politics deter good candidates from standing	25	3
6	Stirring up of political feeling harmful	23½	6
7	Councillor selection in safe wards in hands of majority party	20	2
8	Local elections used to keep party machine in trim	15½	2

The argument which appealed most to respondents both in terms of the number of first preferences obtained was the statement that 'The activities of local councils are not basically of a party political nature'. This statement may appear to be a tautology; one is against party politics in local government because party politics has no place in local government. In fact, a large number of ratepayer activists do seem to think in this way. For many of them, party politics in local government 'should be right out' or 'absolutely right out'; its exclusion is for them a fundamental canon of political life which cannot be the subject of further deliberation. However, this statement also appealed to those respondents who felt that party politics had 'little bearing on local things which happen'. As one respondent put it, 'If you want to decide whether to build a new road or repair an old one, you need common sense'.

The argument which received the second largest number of points was the statement that 'The party group system has a harmful effect on the working of local councils by making debates in the council chamber meaningless'. This concern with open decision-making is reflected in the evidence of ratepayer movements to the Redcliffe-Maud Commission; considerable stress was laid on the desirability of opening more council committee meetings to the press and public. This seems to be linked with a common fear among ratepayer movements that a great deal goes on in local councils which the public does not but should know about; the demand for new measures on councillors' business interests expressed in the evidence of some rate-payers' associations to the Redcliffe-Maud Commission may be another reflection of this fear. [15] Apart from this preference for a visible local decision-making process, there seemed to be some concern among the activists that were interviewed that existing arrangements severely impaired the quality of the decision-making process in local government. For example, one respondent commented, 'I mostly object (to the fact that) the parties have secret meetings and the voting of the agenda is cut-and-dried, this permits party politicians of a low calibre'. A brief in the existence of the rational voter is a core assumption of many of the arguments against party politics in local government [16] and it is presumably difficult for such an individual to make an appropriate judgement on local affairs if the most important political debates are conducted behind closed doors.

Although the 'open debate' argument takes second place among the list of statements in terms of the number of points scored, the second place in terms of expressed first preferences is taken by the argument that 'The regular stirring up of political feeling in the local community is harmful'. This argument, however, takes sixth place in terms of the number of points scored. In other words, it was accorded high priority by a minority of respondents, but the majority of respondents did not even allocate it a second or third preference rating. For a small subgroup of activists, the feat that party politics was associated with a rise in levels of conflict was a real and important one. As one respondent put it, 'Party politics tend to start too many arguments'.

The third most popular argument in terms of points scored was that 'Party politics leads to the adoption of doctrinnaire policies regardless of individual circumstances'. In general, respondents seemed more concerned with arguments about the effect of party politics on the quality of the decision-making process (e.g., the concern about 'meaningless' debates) or on the quality of policy outputs (e.g., 'doctrinnaire policies') than with arguments about its effect on the way in which elections are conducted. The argument that 'Party politics often deter people who would make good councillors from standing for the council' had a certain appeal (it was 4= in terms of points scored and 3rd in terms of preferences), but it should be noted that some councillors perceived a link between the calibre of councillors and the quality of council decisions. However, respondents were not greatly concerned with the impact of party politics on the electoral process in local government either in terms of the way in which candidates were selected or the effect of party politics on the nature of the election campaign. The arguments that 'Where a ward has a clear majority one way or the other for a particular party, the election of a councillor is virtually in the hands of the committee of that party' and 'Local elections are used simply as a means of keeping the party machine in trim and local issues are disregarded' occupied the bottom two rankings in terms of points scored and expressed first preferences. Respondents did not seem particularly concerned about who chose candidates or how the campaign was organised as long as councillors were responsive to public opinion once they were elected.

What should be stressed is the strength and emotional intensity with which the respondents condemned party politics in local government. Although the basic theme that emerged was that party politics was irrelevant to the concerns of local government and unhelpful for the process of local decision-making, respondents also seemed to be giving vent to a wider distaste for politics in general.

Both ratepayer activists and independent councillors would appear to be strongly opposed to party politics in local government. However, is this attitude confined to a vocal minority or does it extend to the public in general? In an attempt to answer this question, a secondary analysis was undertaken of a sample survey of 786 electors carried out in Eastleigh, Hampshire, in 1969. [17] Eastleigh was, at the time of the study, a non-county borough outside Southampton where party political intervention in local elections had first taken place in the 1930's. Despite this, the majority of respondents thought that there should not be party politics on local councils.

Table 4.2
Whether there should be party politics on local councils

Yes	25.8%	204
No	63.9%	501
Don't know	10.3%	81
	100%	786

When asked for their reasons for their replies, 29.9 per cent of respondents said that they would prefer to vote for the individual. 16.7 per cent agreed with the statement that 'Local government should be left to the experts/officials'. 13.9 per cent though that 'Party politics may not be good for the community' and 6.6 per cent thought that 'Party politics doesn't let ordinary people have a real say'. On the other hand, 13.2 per cent of respondents thought 'It's more efficient when you know what party they are' and 8.3 per cent were of the view that 'Party politics lets ordinary people take part'.

Ninety-nine independent variables were used in an attempt to locate any subgroups in the sample which might be particularly hostile, or particularly favourable to party politics in local government. In fact, a majoirty of all the subgroups analysed were opposed to party politics in local government (the only exception was a small group of 23 respondents who said that they preferred the area they lived in because it was a better class area). Council tenants were as opposed to party politics as owner occupiers; trade union membership made no difference to attitudes; nor did length of education. Length of residence and interest in the area did not have any impact on attitudes to party politics in local government.

Nevertheless, there were some independent variables included in the analysis which did help to explain why respondents were supporters or opponents of party politics in local government. A small sample survey carrid out by the author in a nonpartisan area in Devon [18] found that Liberal voters were more strongly opposed to party politics in local government than Conservatives and that Labour voters were less strongly opposed to party intervention than the supporters of the other two parties. This pattern was replicated in the Eastleigh data.

Table 4.3
Attitude towards party politics in local government and vote in last general election

Attitude towards party politics	Conservative	Labour	Liberal
Yes	24.2%	28.8%	18.6%
No	69.8%	59.8%	76.7%
Don't know	6.0%	11.4%	4.7%
	100%	100%	100%
	(285)	(264)	(43)

Furthermore, if one considers the subgroup of Labour supporters (118) who claimed to have voted in the preceding town council election, 37.3 per cent said that they were in favour of party politics in local government and 49.2 per cent were opposed. Not surprisingly, social class variables also have some explanatory value. As far as self-assessed class was concerned, there was little variation in the levels of support and opposition for party politics in local government among those respondents designating themselves 'upper middle', 'middle', 'lower middle' or 'skilled working'. However, a higher proportion of those respondents designating themselves 'unskilled working class' (35.1 per cent of 57 respondents) supported party politics in local government.

If one considers occupation of respondent and occupation of head of household, the two groups which are most favourable to party politics in local government are Registrar General's Social Classes 1 and 5, although the proportion of 'don't knows' is much higher in Social Class 5 than in Social Class 1. The highest levels of opposition to party politics in local government are recorded in Social Class 2, although it must be stressed that the differences are relatively small ones.

Table 4.4
Attitude towards party politics in local government by occupation of respondent

Attitude towards party politics	Registrar-General's Social Class				
	One	Two	Three	Four	Five
Yes	30.4%	22.1%	21.0%	26.8%	29.1%
No	65.2%	73.5%	70.1%	65.5%	54.0%
Don't know	4.3%	4.4%	9.0%	7.7%	16.9%
	99.9%	100%	100.1%	100%	100%
	(46)	(113)	(167)	(194)	(261)

Table 4.5
Attitude towards party politics in local government by occupation of head of household

Attitude towards party politics	One	Two	Three	Four	Five
Yes	32.0%	24.6%	18.4%	27.0%	32.0%
No	64.0%	66.7%	63.2%	59.0%	51.0%
Don't know	4.0%	8.8%	18.4%	14.0%	17.0%
	100%	100.1%	100%	100%	100%
	(25)	(57)	(76)	(100)	(100)

The results on social class may help to explain why Roman Catholic respondents were more likely to favour party politics in local government (34.8 per cent of 46 respondents) than Church of England or Nonconformist respondents. Age made some difference to the pattern of responses in so far as respondents under 34 were more likely to support party politics in local government (30.2 per cent of 199 respondents) than older respondents. However, the intergenerational differences were not substantial and there was no indication that opposition to party politics in local government was a relic of socialisation into politics at a time when party intervention in local politics was less widespread. Indeed, the group most strongly opposed to party politics in local government was the 35—44 age group (72.5 per cent of all respondents).

The data did indicate that respondents' attitudes towards party politics in local government might be affected by their exposure to particular kinds of local political system. Respondents who had lived in Greater London were less likely to be opposed to party politics in local government than those who had lived in less partisan areas (particularly Hampshire outside the Southampton area and the rest of the South of England).

Table 4.6

Attitude towards party politics in local government by previous area of residence

Attitude towards party politics	Previous area of residence		
	Greater London	Southampton/ Eastleigh	Rest of Hants./ South of England
Yes	34.2%	27.7%	20.0%
No	50.0%	60.2%	53.3%
Don't know	15.8%	12.1%	26.7%
	100%	100%	100%
	(38)	(256)	(60)

One of the most significant differences in the pattern of responses was between those respondents who thought that a change of party control of the local council made a difference and those who thought it made no difference. As one might expect, those respondents who thought that a change of power made a difference were more favourable to party politics in local government than those who thought that a change of power made no difference.

Table 4.7

Attitude towards party politics in local government by attitude towards change of control of local council

Attitude towards party politics	Change of control		
	Makes difference	Does not	Don't know
Yes	33.4%	20.2%	20.0%
No	59.6%	69.1%	53.3%
Don't know	7.0%	10.7%	26.7%
	100%	100%	100%
	(344)	(382)	(60)

Similarly, those respondents who thought that council officials ran the town were less likely to support party politics in local government (19.0 per cent of 58 respondents) than those who thought that the councillors (27.9 per cent of 219 respondents) or the political parties (28.2 per cent of 78 respondents) ran the town. In general, then, it would seem that electors who have more confidence in the efficacy of democratic control in local government are more likely to support party politics in local government. One should add that the flow of causation may run in the other direction; electors who support party intervention in local government may believe, as a consequence, that such intervention is in some sense efficacious.

Although analysis of the data indicated that some subgroups in the population (e.g., the unskilled working class and Labour voters) are more likely to be well disposed to party politics in local government than other subgroups, the picture that emerges is of a general opposition (in Eastleigh, at any rate) to party politics in local government among all social categories. Nevertheless, the electors of Eastleigh had returned, in the years preceding the study, a predominantly party political council. In particular, independent and ratepayer representatives had been replaced by Conservatives. This would seem to suggest that the respondents' views on party politics in local government were not strongly held. However, this latent opposition of party politics in local government can be mobilised in specific circumstances. A ratepayers' organisation campaigning on a specific issue may also appeal to electors' distaste for party politics in local government. For example, in Eastleigh in the 1960's a residents' association fighting a compulsory redevelopment scheme was able to win three seats in the town's central ward.

The general conclusion that is drawn is that public opposition to party politics in local government does not, of itself, provide a sufficient basis for sustaining a purely local party of the ratepayer type. However, in combination with other factors, electors' distaste for party politics in local government can be used to help to create support for a purely local party. At the very least, even if electors are not as vehemently opposed to party politics in local government as some ratepayer activists, they would not appear to be particularly enthusiastic supporters of party intervention.

Concern about the alleged inquiries of the rating system is certainly not confined to ratepayer activists. A study of public attitudes to local government finance supervised by the Government Social Survey found that 'significantly fewer people agree that rating is a fair system than agree the same about VAT or income tax'. [19] Rating seems to attract an unpopularity out of all proportion to all its impact on household incomes. In fact, only thirteen per cent of the income of local authorities in England and Wales in 1975/6 came from domestic rates. [20] In 1975 only 1.9 per cent of gross household incomes in Great Britain was spent on rates, compared with 15.9 per cent on income tax and 14.5 per cent on national indirect taxes. [21]

Two factors would seem to contribute to the unpopularity of what is, in terms of its impact on the budget of the average household, a relatively minor tax. First, there is considerable public ignorance about a number of important aspects of the rating system. The Government Social Survey found that 'over half of all adults have no knowledge of the basic method of calculating rate bills' [22] and only 'about a quarter of all adults (and slightly more heads of household) can recall their actual rate bills to within ten per cent of the correct amount'. [23] Although most respondents knew that the Government contributes to local government finance, 'only eighteen per cent of adults in England and Wales know, within a range of plus or minus fifty per cent what the approximate figure for the Government grant in their area is'. [24] Most respondents underestimated the size of the Government contribution. Only nine per cent of adult respondents were aware that both upper and lower tier authorities are responsible for levying rates. [25] It was also found that 'Those most critical of the rating system tend also to be those who know most about it. They include mainly people who own their homes and are in professional, managerial and other non-manual occupations or are self-employed'. [26] This last finding has important political implications. This group of well informed individuals who are highly critical of the rating system, and who come from occupations in which they are likely to have acquired basic organisational skills, from a pool from which the activists of ratepayer movements are likely to be drawn. In so far as public understanding of the rating system tends to make it appear more unfair than it actually is, those individuals who are critical of the rating system are likely to have a receptive public audience for their message.

Moreover, in attempting to arouse public indignation about the rating system, they are likely to be helped by the second of the major factors which contributes to the unpopularity of the rating system. Even if the majority of the electorate do not understand the way in which rates are determined, they are often aware that they are (for example) paying more rates than a workmate doing the same job. As the Layfield Report points out. 'The amount of rates paid by people in similar circumstances in similar accommodation varies very widely between areas.' [27] Moreover, 'the circumstances of people may vary widely although they live in houses which quite properly bear the same rating assessment'. [28] Although this 'variation is less marked if the burden of rating is considered over a family's lifetime'. [29] this is little consolation to the householder trying to balance the family budget. As the Layfield Report somewhat drily observes, 'At any time, rating will be a much heavier burden on income for some people than for others, which has consequences for the overall tolerability of the level of rating.' [30] Undoubtedly, rates do have 'considerable merits as a local tax', [31] but the average ratepayer is unlikely to study the arguments followed by the Layfield Report to reach this conclusion. What is likely to concern him is the impact of the system on his own personal financial circumstances. Between 1974 and 1975, when ratepayer agitation was at its height, there were some fairly wide variations in the relationship between rate changes and income changes: over 25 per cent of households had percentage increases in rates at least double their income changes'. [32] If one combines the indignation of individual householders over changes of this sort with the arguments of ratepayer activists that the rating system offends basic notions of justice, it is not difficult to account for the growth of ratepayer movements during and after 1974.

Nevertheless, the incidence and success of ratepayer movements since 1974 has varied considerably from one place to another. In many places, the Conservative Party has capitalised on the indignation of ratepayers. It is argued that ratepayer movements are particularly likely to be successful in areas where the Conservative Party is relatively weak. This argument is borne out if one examines the results of the 1976 district council elections. In England, ratepayer candidates took 36 seats from Labour. Independents lost 35 seats to ratepayers, but the Conservatives lost only five seats to ratepayers and the Liberals one. The picture was even more striking in Wales where ratepayers took fifty-three seats from Labour. On seven authorities, the ratepayers made gains from Labour where no Conservatives (or only one) were returned. In part, of course, this was a reaction against what was termed 'arrogance and complacency that resulted from decades of Labour supremacy and has made local government look disreputable'. [33] However, it is interesting that this reaction took the form in many areas of electoral support for ratepayer rather than Conservative candidates. In Swansea, the Ratepayers gained seats from the Conservatives as well as Labour to take control of the council, although special local factors influenced the result.

Nevertheless, it may require particularly high rate rises for a ratepayer movement to be really successful electorally. The greatest successes of ratepayer candidates in English metropolitan districts have been in Wakefield and Barnsley. In 1974 these experienced the largest rate rises of any of the new metropolitan districts (105.3 per cent in the case of Wakefield and 98.3 per cent in the case of Barnsley). [34] Rate rises of this magnitude may overcome political inertia among the electorate and attachment to existing party loyalties, although it is difficult to specify a point at which rate rises become politically intolerable. Particular local issues may help ratepayers, but since 1974 ratepayer candidates have sometimes been successful in the absence of any particular local grievance. For example, in the 1976 district council elections, ratepayer candidates took three seats from independents in the Alcester wards of Stratford District. There were no particular local issues; a well organised ratepayer movement simply aroused the electorate's indignation about the rating system and levels of local government expenditure.

As was pointed out in earlier chapters, pre-reorganisation ratepayer movements were often the outcome of conflicts arising from the character of particular local political systems. Particularly in the case of the resort town, these conflicts did not easily exhaust themselves. New issues were always bringing to the surface the underlying tension between ratepayer and trader interests. The pre-reorganisation ratepayer movements, at least in some cases, enjoyed some kind of social base which remained after particular issues had been resolved. Many of the post-reorganisation movements arose out of a general discontent with the rating system which was not confined to any particular locality. However, the initial tide of indignation quickly evaporated and the post-reorganisation movements are likely to prove ephemeral. The remainder of the chapter is devoted to an examination of a particular post-reorganisation ratepayer movement in an attempt to explore the bases of support and chances of survival, of such organisations.

One of the distinguishing characteristics of the ratepayer movements which were formed during the 'ratepayers' revolt' of 1974 was that they were not confined to the predominantly middle class areas in which ratepayer movements had previously tended to flourish. Many of the new movements were in Labour-dominated industrial areas in the Midlands and the North of England. This case study looks at one such ratepayer movement, that which developed in the metropolitan borough of Walsall in the West Midlands.

The Walsall Metropolitan District was formed from a merger of the Walsall County Borough and the Aldridge-Brownhills Urban District. The three constituencies in the area all returned Labour Members of Parliament in 1974, although both Walsall South and Aldridge-Brownhills were won by small majorities and Walsall North was subsequently lost to the Conservatives in a by-election. In the initial elections for the new metropolitan district in 1973, ratepayer activity was confined to the Streetly Ward in Aldridge-Brownhills where three ratepayer candidates were returned without Conservative opposition. However, by the time of the 1975 elections, the Streetly organisation had been joined by two new ratepayer movements based in Walsall and in Aldridge. Ratepayer candidates fought twelve of the twenty wards in the metropolitan district in 1975, winning three and increasing their representation on the council to five members. In 1976 they fought only six seats, but they won three of these, increasing their total strength on the council to seven. Their 1976 successes gave them, in effect, the balance of power on the Walsall Metropolitan District Council which was then composed of 28 Labour councillors; 19 Conservatives; 7 Ratepayers; 4 Independents; 1 Liberal; and 1 Independent Labour.

It is difficult to explain the pattern of success of the Ratepayer movement in Walsall because their nominations for council seats have displayed a 'formlessness' similar to that noted by Stanyer during a period of ratepayer activity in Exeter. [35] One factor in the situation has been the determination of the three ratepayer organisations to maintain their independence from one another. In the run-up to the 1976 elections, a leading Ratepayer councillor insisted that 'I must make it clear that Walsall, Streetly and Aldridge Ratepayers are three separate organisations and it is vital that they remain so', although he conceded that 'as it seems certain that Ratepayer councillors will hold the balance of power from May 7, council links become inevitable'. [36]

Six of the seven seats held by Ratepayers are in the old Aldridge-Brownhills area. They held in 1976 all three seats in the Streetly ward (two won against Conservative opposition) and have taken two seats in Aldridge North and South from the Conservatives. Their one seat in Walsall proper (Bloxwich East) was taken from Labour in 1975 without the Conservatives putting forward a candidate. In 1976 there was no Ratepayer candidate and the Labour candidate defeated his Conservative opponent. The other Ratepayer seat is in Brownhills Central. In 1975 this seat was taken by Labour, although the combined Conservative and Ratepayer vote outnumbered the Labour vote by 1,258 to 969. This arithmetic does not appear to have escaped the local Conservatives, for in 1976 the Ratepayer candidate had no Conservative opponent. The Ratepayer vote was just twelve more (1,270) than the combined Conservative and Ratepayer total in the preceding year; the extra fifteen votes won by Labour were, of course, not enough for them to save the seat.

These successes aside, there are many wards in which Ratepayer candidates have attracted a relatively small proportion of the vote. In what kinds of wards have the Ratepayers been most successful? In an attempt to answer this question, a series of aggregate data measures for each ward were obtained from the 1971 census ward library. Walsall has three distinctively middle class wards. Five of the seven Ratepayer councillors have been elected from two of these wards, Streetly and Aldridge North and South. The Ratepayers contested the other middle class ward, Paddock, which is in Walsall, in 1975 but received only 19.1 per cent of the vote; they did not contest Paddock in 1976. The Ratepayers have done moderately well in the ward which ranks fourth in terms of socio-economic grouping of head of household, Hatherton, where they received 34.1 per cent of the vote in 1975 and 33.3 per cent in 1976. Only one other ward has over 30 per cent of heads of households in non-manual socio-economic groupings (St. Matthews) and that ward contains an unusually high proportion of households in unfurnished rented accommodation.

Table 4.8

Ratepayer share of the vote and ward socio-economic composition in Walsall
(ranked by non-manual heads of household)

Ward	Percentage owner-occupied households	Non-manual heads of household	Non-manual persons	Ratepayer vote 1975	1976
Paddock (Walsall)	82.7%	67.2%	65.3%	19.1%	—
Streetly (Aldridge-Brownhills)	93.5%	63.4%	66.0%	50.9%	47.4%
Aldridge North and South	66.6%	46.2%	48.1%	53.6%	55.0%
Hatherton (Walsall)	38.5%	36.3%	36.7%	34.1%	33.3%

*Non-manual is defined terms of the percentage of the category in Registrar-General's socio-economic groups one to six (farmers are an insignificant category in Walsall).

It would therefore seem that the Ratepayers have been most successful in non-manual seats in the old Aldridge-Brownhills Urban District; certainly it is only in this area that they have won seats against Conservative opposition. Apart from the issue of rate increases, the Ratepayers have voiced concern about the way in which the Aldridge area has been developed, expressing worries that it has lost its 'character' during rapid expansion. The other two Ratepayer victories have been won (admittedly without Conservative opposition) in areas which would not normally be regarded as propitious for Ratepayer activity. In Brownhills Central, 60.8 per cent of households live in council properties, but the Ratepayers managed to secure

56.3 per cent of the vote in 1976. In Bloxwich East, 72.1 per cent of households live in council properties, but the Ratepayers managed to secure 56.9 per cent of the vote in 1975; moreover, the Conservatives failed to win the seat from Labour in the absence of a Ratepayer candidate in 1976. It has been observed that owner occupiers are 'more likely to favour the Conservatives in areas of high working class composition than in more middle class areas' [37] and it may be that the Rate-payers drew disproportionate support in these wards from the minority of electors who were owner-occupiers. However, the Ratepayers must have attracted a considerable proportion of their support from council tenants.

Both Brownhills Central and Bloxwich East are relatively prosperous wards, measured in terms of the access of households to a car. Indeed, the Ratepayers have not won a seat in a ward where less than half of the population has access to a car apart from Bloxwich East, and there 47.5 per cent of households have access to a car. Indeed, although the Ratepayers have contested five of the eight wards in which sixty per cent or more of households do not have access to a car, they have never won more than 26 per cent of the vote in any of these wards. The Walsall data suggests that ratepayer candidates can attract support from both owner occupiers and council tenants and from non-manual and manual workers. The groups which are least likely to give them support are the least prosperous sections of the electorate. In a sense, this is a rational outcome, as these are the groups which are likely to lose most from the cuts in expenditure advocated by ratepayer movements, although it is not implied that voters have made that kind of calculation.

The electoral appeals of the ratepayers' organisations in Walsall are centred on curbing local government expenditure, combined with an emphasis on the supposed inadequacies of party political representation. In February 1976, the chairman of the Aldridge Ratepayer's Association stated, 'There is enough bureaucratic control in this country without creating further local government empires and monopolies. What is local government about? It has a splendid role and that role concerns the people of this area, not the whims and power seeking of the parties.' [38] Similarly, in the 1976 election campaign, a Ratepayer councillor declared that he favoured 'cutting waste and spending plus stricter financial control'. [39] Ratepayer councillors were simply 'there for the people'. [40]

The results of the 1976 elections placed the Ratepayers on a potentially influential position on the council. It had been stressed before the election that 'Ratepayer councillors enjoy the freedom to vote against one another as their conscience dictates'. [41] Immediately after the elections, the Labour group called a special council meeting at which they placed a 'policy package' before the council covering the main policies pursued by Labour over the preceding three years. A Tory amendment that the package 'lie on the table' was seconded by a Ratepayer councillor and carried by 30 votes to 29 with all the Ratepayer and Independent councillors voting with the Conservatives, although the solitary Liberal voted against the Conservative amendment. Subsequently, the Conservatives and Ratepayers joined together to appoint committee chairmen, although the Conservative leader stated that there was no coalition between the two groups. The Ratepayers subsequently supported a special autumn rates rise of 3p in the £, although this was combined with additional spending cuts of £308,000. In March 1977 a rents rise was carried by the Conservatives and Ratepayers against Labour opposition.

What the preceding case study shows is that it is possible for a ratepayer movement to gather considerable support from a broad cross-section of the electorate in the absence of any specific local issue which has aroused general indignation. An emphasis on cutting local government expenditure and on keeping party politics out of local government would seem to be a formula that can win votes, particularly from the more prosperous sections of the electorate and in areas which have been incorporated in larger local authority areas as a result of reorganisation.

In many ways, winning elections is the least of a ratepayer movement's problems. One should not exaggerate the organisational and political skills which are needed to mount a reasonably effective local election campaign. The real difficulties start when the movement has elected some councillors. In the course of the case studies of pre-organisation movements reported in Chapter Three, it was often found that the ethic of independence adhered to by these movements led to problems in relations between the councillors and the movement. Often, councillors would modify their views as a result of the new perspectives they acquired in the course of their council work. If the association complained, the councillors pointed out that they have been elected on a platform of acting in accordance with the dictates of their conscience. Post-reorganisation movements are likely to face similar problems. If ratepayer councillors are a minority on a council, it is difficult for them to do more than to publicise their members' grievances and possibly to use their access to information to uncover examples of council 'waste' or 'extravagence'. If the tides of electoral fortune place them in a position where they hold the balance of power between the parties, their abhorrence of political deals makes it difficult for them to make the most of their position (although it is surprising how quickly ratepayer groups acquire political skills when the situation requires it). Political parties may be reluctant to enter into a coalition arrangement with a group that does not 'whip' its members, although it is surprising how often the dictates of conscience and an examination of the merits of the issue lead ratepayer councillors to vote in the same way. Perhaps the major constraint that a ratepayer group faces is that it is difficult to see how an organisation calling for cuts in local government expenditure on a substantial scale could enter into an arrangement with a group of Labour councillors. Indeed, in some cases, ratepayer councillors may form a right-wing or populist opposition to the Conservatives. For example at Worthing in 1973, where the Ratepayers took twelve district council seats, the President of Worthing Ratepayers declared: 'How low has the (Conservative) Association sunk from the principles of the true blue Conservative party . . . They cannot be relied upon to follow Conservative principles or policies'.

Local government reorganisation has meant that the kinds of local conflict discussed in Chapters Two and Three are less likely to lead to the formation of purely local parties, although this is not to say that they may not play a role in local party formation in certain circumstances. However, purely local parties of the

101

ratepayer type now rely much more on grievances about the rating system and the role of party politics in local government which are not confined to particular localities. This is not to say that local considerations are irrelevant. A particularly high rate increase may serve to focus electors' grievances about the rating system; the way in which a council handles a particular local issue may revive electors' distaste for party politics in local government. If a purely local party does form, its success may depend to a considerable extent on the strength of the local branches of the national political parties. In 1976 ratepayer candidates did particularly well where the Conservative Party was weak or where independent candidates were unable to cope with a vigorous ratepayer challenge which followed years of elections which were either uncontested or fought in a low key.

It is very unusual for a ratepayer movement to be able to win control of a local authority. Most ratepayer movements start to fall apart long before they reach their goal as the initial euphoria gives way to a realisation of the limits of what can be achieved, a decline often hastened by personality clashes. Perhaps their greatest impact on the local political system comes through the influence that their existence has on other councillors who fear that they may lose their seats, or fail to win seats from their party political opponents, because of a ratepayer intervention. For example, in Eastleigh, the successful residents' intervention in one ward confirmed the belief of Labour councillors 'that they must remain firmly in touch with ward opinion'. [42] The importance of ratepayer movements cannot be measured simply in terms of the number of council seats they hold; their greatest impact is through the influence that their existence (or even the possibility of their existence) exerts on the minds of councillors. As Newton observes, 'What is important is the subjective feeling of council members that their own actions and policies do matter, and that voters do hold them accountable on polling day.' [43] It is by reinforcing such 'subjective feelings' that ratepayer movements continue to play an important role in English and Welsh local politics.

Notes

[1] *Local Government Chronicle,* 28 June 1974.
[2] *Report on the Committee of Enquiry on Local Government Finance (Layfield Report),* Cmnd.6453, HMSO, London 1976, p.354..
[3] Ibid., p.26.
[4] Evidence of the National Union of Ratepayers' Associations to the Layfield Committee, p.104.
[5] *Sunday Times,* 30 June 1974.
[6] *Local Government Chronicle,* 3 January 1975.
[7] D. Moller, 'When Ratepayers Turn Watchdogs', *Reader's Digest,* vol.108, no.649, May 1976, pp.44–48, p.45.
[8] Evidence of the National Association of Ratepayer Action Groups to the Layfield Committee, p.96.

[9] Ibid., p.103.

[10] *The Economist,* 30 November 1975.

[11] *Report of the Committee on the Management of Local Government,* HMSO, London 1967, p.109.

[12] *Royal Commission on Local Government in England, Written Evidence of Private Citizens, Amenity, Ratepayers' and Residents' Associations and Other Witnesses,* HMSO, London 1969, p.418.

[13] R.C. Wood, *Suburbia: Its People and Their Politics,* Houghton Miffin, Boston 1963, p.155.

[14] M. Kesselman, *The Ambiguous Consensus,* Knopf, New York 1967, p.136.

[15] *Royal Commission on Local Government in England, Other Witnesses,* op.cit., p.410, 441, 537.

[16] Wood, op. cit., p.155.

[17] D.M. Hill and I. Robinson, *Politics and Local Life: a Study of the Borough and Constituency of Eastleigh,* Social Science Research Council Report HR 472, 1972.

[18] See W.P. Grant, 'Nonpartisanship in British Local Politics', *Policy and Politics,* vol.1, no.1, 1973, pp.241–66.

[19] Layfield Report, op.cit., p.366.

[20] Ibid., p.377.

[21] Ibid., p.432.

[22] Ibid., p.365.

[23] Ibid., p.366.

[24] Layfield Report, *Survey of Attitudes to Local Government Finance,* microfiche edition, p.23.

[25] Ibid., p.23.

[26] Layfield Report, op.cit., p.367.

[27] Ibid., p.258.

[28] Ibid., p.258.

[29] Ibid., p.258.

[30] Ibid., p.258.

[31] Ibid., p.259.

[32] Ibid., p.434.

[33] *The Times,* 8 May 1976.

[34] *Rates and Rateable Values in England and Wales, 1974-5,* HMSO, London 1976.

[35] J. Stanyer, 'Exeter' in L.J. Sharpe (ed.), *Voting in Cities,* Macmillan, London 1967, pp.112–131, p.119.

[36] *Walsall Observer,* 30 April 1976.

[37] P. Garrahan, 'Housing, The Class Milieu and Middle-Class Conservatism', *British Journal of Political Science,* vol.7, no.1, January 1977, pp.126 -127, p.127.

[38] *Walsall Observer,* 6 February 1976.

[39] Ibid., 30 April 1976.

[40] Ibid., 9 April 1976.

[41] Ibid., 9 April 1976.

[42] K. Newton, *Second City Politics,* Oxford University Press, London 1976, p.21.

Conclusions

Newton has argued, 'National political considerations beyond the reach and control of local politicians seem to determine local election outcomes, and local factors, whether in the form of local issues or the record and policies of local candidates and parties, seem to have slight impact'. [1] This observation may apply to many areas, particularly the big cities, but the persistence of independent councillors and ratepayer movements as local political phenomena suggest that it is not the case everywhere. Even a fully partisan system may be open to all kinds of local influences: electors may discriminate between candidates; local political parties may take a view which is contrary to that of their national leadership but seems to them to be in the interests of the locality they serve. For example, in Eastleigh, a community where party politics became dominant before the Second World War, the controlling Labour group displayed an 'intense localism' and continued right up to the mid 1960's, the wider (and in some ways more flexible) approach of the initial style of the Independents'. [2] As Newton emphasises, 'local politics are not simply national politics writ small'. [3] Nevertheless, 'the defence of localism has undoubtedly become more difficult in recent years'. [4] The persistence of independent and ratepayer councillors are signs of a continuing resistance to the 'nationalisation' of local politics, of a continuing adherence to a rhetoric of nonpartisanship, but for how long can they survive?

In order to answer this question, it is necessary to emphasise that the two principal local political phenomena studied in this book—independent councillors and purely local political movements of the ratepayer type—are different in a number of significant ways. Independent councillors are deeply rooted in a tightly-knit local social structure; they are the political expression of a particular kind of social system. It is a system continually under threat from pressures from economic and social change. It is perhaps not surprising that independent politics is at its strongest in those parts of the country which are geographically distant from the metropolis and which enjoy a distinct communal identity (Cornwall and the west of Wales). Ratepayer movements flourish in a rather different kind of environment. They are the product of political indignation rather than the outcome of the politics of cohesive communities. Independent councillors stand (symbolically at any rate) for the perpetuation of a traditional pattern of politics; ratepayers challenge a pattern of politics which they have come to distrust. The independent councillors enjoy a stronger social base than the ratepayers; the ratepayers, on the other hand, can draw on a sense of political indignation which is not dependent on the survival of a particular kind of local society.

What brings these rather disparate phenomena together is their shared adherence to the linked ideologies of nonpartisanship and localism. As Elliott et al. have pointed out, 'An ideology of nonpartisanship exists and has deep roots in the political development of (Britain) and any attempt to trace it out quickly reveals how tightly it has been linked to sets of ideas which stress the importance of autonomy, to the insistence that towns and cities could and should be run by local people, for local people—in short to "localism".' [5]

Although there has been something of an intellectual (and a political) reaction against 'bigness' and centralisation in recent years, the underlying economic and social forces which create a tendency towards the centralisation of government and politics are still at work. Complex technology tends to enhance the value of professional, as compared with local, knowledge; similarly, the geographically mobile (over represented in the more politically active middle class) are likely to prefer conformity rather than diversity in the provision of services. There are pressures in the other direction. for example, there is an increasing interest in 'alternative' technologies. However, in the view of Elliott et al., 'local politics can no longer be so "local" nor so "nonpartisan"; both the ideologies and the personnel have significantly changed'. [6] The rational-managerialist forces which produced local government reorganisation overcame the localist forces which saw reorganis-ation as a threat to the civic expression of the values of the small place.

Is 'localism' a dying force which is doomed to a lingering death on the western fringes of England and Wales, enlivened by an occasional outburst of ratepayer activity in the more urbanised areas? 'Localism' is associated with a vivid rhetoric, centred around beliefs in the value of 'community' and an emotive, but not particularly well articulated, distaste for party politics in local government. It is often a rhetoric with a ring of despair; for example, as one 'Westward' councillor noted in a debate on some proposals from the Local Government Boundary Commission, 'We do not want to be taxed, rated, cheated and thieved against, as has been happening for so long. What we want to do is to . . . govern our own locality without interference from Whitehall'.

Many party councillors would like to see less central government interference, but 'localism' is more than a view about central-local relations; it is, as Young has stated, "the emotive symbolisation of the values of the small place'. [7] However, emotive rhetoric is not enough to safeguard 'localist' values; political leverage is also necessary. Bulpitt has argued that independent politics has 'represented the politics of territorial defence—the defence of the local community from outside, particularly central, forces'. [8] One result, in Bulpitt's view, has been the obstruc-tion of any major linkage between central and local politics, 'something generally regarded as a basic feature of political activity in developed western systems'. [9] Bulpitt thus draws attention to one of the paradoxes of 'localism', the fact that its encouragement of an insulation of local politics from national politics conducted in the capital city has left a vacuum which makes the very centralisation which 'localists' oppose easier to achieve.

'Localists' values are not confined to independent councillors and purely local parties, but they are the most vigorous defenders of such values. Their presence in local politics is a constant reminder that local politics is something more than a reflection of national politics. In the absence of these phenomena, localist values might well survive in the local branches of the national political parties, but they would have to contend with other sets of values which are national in orientation.

Any prognosis of the chances of survival of 'localist' values must take account of two somewhat unpredictable considerations. The first is the future of local government finance. The Layfield Report on Local Government Finance saw the choice for the future as being one between central responsibility and local responsibility. As the Report points out, 'If the government assumed the main responsibility for local government expenditure, it would set the totals for local spending within fairly narrow limits. It would have to determine how much each authority was to spend and for what purpose.' [10] In this situation, localist values would become more and more a matter of rhetoric and less and less a matter of political reality. Independent councillors might come to the view that it would be more expedient to join a national political party in an attempt to exert influence at the centre rather than to concentrate on the diminishing range of purely local decisions. Ratepayer councillors would find it even more difficult to influence the income and expenditure patterns of local authorities and hence even more difficult to justify their conduct to their supporters.

On the other hand, greater local responsibility would involve allowing 'local authorities greater freedom to decide their own priorities and act accordingly'. [11] The independent councillors might find that the political parties would take a greater interest in the activities of local councils which had more influence over policy outputs in such key areas as housing. However, much would depend on the electorate's attitude towards party politics in local government and, in particular, the intensity of the electorate's beliefs on this subject in the areas at present controlled by independents. Layfield suggests that under a system involving greater local responsibility, 'all authorities should continue to levy both domestic and non-domestic rates and . . . the major spending authority in each area should also levy Local Income Tax'. [12] The reduced role for domestic rates would partly satisfy one of the major grievances of ratepayer movements. On the other hand, greater local autonomy might encourage greater public interest in the activities of local government. Ratepayer movements might re-style themselves 'LIT' (Local Income Tax) movements, but their range of concern and political orientation would be much the same. A great deal will depend on the precise nature of the solution eventually introduced. For example, if some of the more expensive services were simply transferred from local government to central government, a solution not favoured by Layfield but preferred by some politicians, local pressures in the form of ratepayer movements would tend to diminish.

The second consideration is that of electoral reform. The movement for the introduction of some form of proportional representation has developed sufficient momentum for it at least to be considered as a possible future development. Of course, most of the debate on this subject has been concerned with central (and European) rather than local government, but the introduction of a system of proportional representation at a national level would presumably be followed by its introduction at the local level (although it might be permissive rather than mandatory for local authorities). [13] Similarly, the introduction of proportional representation for European elections or for elections to Scottish or Welsh assemblies might also stimulate interest in its introduction for local government elections. [14] Much would depend on the system of proportional representation used. A 'party list' system would hasten the demise of the independent councillor; an 'independent slate', although possible, would be in conflict with some of the central values of independent councillors. Ratepayer movements might also find it difficult to organise under a list system. However, most commentators seem to prefer some variant of the single transferable vote system. The introduction of a STV system in local government would probably help independent and ratepayer candidates. Voters would not be deterred from voting for such a candidate by the fear of letting an opposition candidate in; if an independent or ratepayer candidate was unsuccessful, his or her votes would (generally) be transferred to the party of each elector's choice at a later stage of the count.

In general, it would seem that the nationalisation of English and Welsh local politics is likely to contine, [15] although the process may take a long time in the remoter parts of the two countries. It is something of a paradox that the political parties are likely to become more dominant in local politics at a time when they are attracting less public support both in terms of the proportion of the electorate who are prepared to vote for them at general elections and the proportion who are prepared to become party members. The picture of the future of local democracy that emerges is in many ways not an attractive one; small local political parties facing an apathetic electorate, given to occasional bursts of 'sporadic intervention', generally of a 'highly individual and unorganised form with affected people arguing against one another for personal compensation and benefit'. [16]

It is easy, of course, to take a sentimental and nostalgic view of 'localism'. Very often it has involved the defence of the interests of a particular section of the community (especially small businessmen) in the name of a more general community interest. Nevertheless, as Young points out, 'The theory of local democracy rests upon certain premises concerning the autonomy of local institutions, the particularity of local circumstances, and the distinctiveness of local political behaviour'. [17] Without that distinctiveness, we may have to think again about what we mean by that much vaunted term. 'local democracy'.

Notes

[1] K. Newton, *Second City Politics,* Oxford University Press, London 1976, p.7.
[2] D.M. Hill and I. Robinson, *Politics and Local Life,* Social Science Research Council Report HR 472, London 1972, p.6.
[3] Newton, op. cit., p.12.
[4] B. Elliott, D. McCrone, V. Skelton, 'Property and Political Power: Edinburgh 1875 to 1975', p.3. Mimeographed paper, Department of Sociology, University of Edinburgh, 1976.

[5] Ibid., p.2.

[6] Ibid., p.17.

[7] K. Young, *Essays on the Study of Urban Politics,* Macmillan, London 1975, p.193.

[8] J.G. Bulpitt, 'English Local Politics: the Collapse of the Ancien Regime?'. Paper delivered to the conference of the Political Studies Association of the United Kingdom, Nottingham, March 1976, p.10.

[9] Ibid., p.10.

[10] *Report of the Committee of Enquiry on Local Government Finance (Layfield Report),* Cmnd.6453, HMSO, London 1976, p.293.

[11] Ibid., p.296.

[12] Ibid., p.294.

[13] For discussions of the question of proportional representation in local government elections see W.P. Grant, 'Electoral Reform and Local Government' in S. Finer (ed.), *Adversary Politics and Electoral Reform,* Anthony Wigram, London 1975, pp.343−59 and B. Keith-Lucas, *Local Elections: Let's Get Them in Proportion,* National Committee for Electoral Reform, London 1977.

[14] It is unlikely that its introduction for local government elections would precede its introduction for other elections.

[15] The outcome in Scotland is less certain. Much would depend on the patterns of politics that developed in a devolved assembly or in an independent nation-state. If independence led to a reversion to a pattern of smaller local government authorities (something which many Nationalists favour), 'localist' forces might be strengthened.

[16] R.E. Dowse and J. Hughes, 'Sporadic Interventionists', *Political Studies,* vol.25, no.1, March 1977, pp.84−92, p.90.

[17] K. Young, *Local Politics and the Rise of Party,* Leicester University Press, Leicester 1975, pp.32−33.

Index

Elliott, McCrone and Skelton 61, 104–5, 107
Ely 56
Essex 37
Established-outsider conflicts 46–47, 50, 56
Exeter 57, 64, 98
Exmouth 56, 82

Farnham Ratepayers' Association 88
France 89

Garrahan, P. 103
'Genuine Local parties' defined 40 *See also* Ratepayers' Associations
Geographical rivalries 17, 34
Gloucester 7
Glyn-Jones, A. 63
Gordon District Council 7
Gwynedd 2, 9
Gyford, J. 4, 5, 7, 38

Hampshire 37
Hampton, W. 7, 65
Havering 4, 76 *See also* Hornchurch
Hawley, W.D. 35, 39
Herefordshire 6
Hereford and Worcester 9
Hertfordshire 37
Hill and Robinson 7, 103, 107
Hillingdon 88
Hjellum, T. 9
Hodges and Smith 64
Holt and Turner 67
Honiton 56
Hornchurch 70, 75
Housing policy 36–37, 72
Humberside 2, 3

Independent councillors: Conservative Party and, 10–13; decline of, 2; informal groupings of, 22; parochial roles of, 26–27; policy-making roles of, 27–28; political

views of, 3, 36–37; pressure groups and, 24–25; rural concentration of, 9–10; unpredictability of, 30–34.
Isle of Wight 2, 7
Isles of Scilly 16

Jackson, A. 48
Jennings, R.E. 3, 7
Jones, G.W. 48

Kammerer, G. 50, 51
Kantor, P. 7
Kastenbaum, R. 64
Keith-Lucas, B. 108
Kent 37
Kesselman, M. 89, 103
Kincardineshire 16, 17, 29
Klapper, J.T. 63

Labour Party: in Billericay, 75; and 'Central' District Council, 11; and Humberside County Council, 2; losses of seats to ratepayers, 97; and tenants' associations, 56; and 'Westward' District Council, 19.
Layfield Report 1, 86, 87, 96, 106
Leamington Spa 57
Lee, J.M. 30, 39, 69
Lee, Wood, Solomon and Walters 12, 37
Leicestershire 37
Le Lohe, M.J. 65
Lewes, Culyer and Brady 64
Liberal Party: in Billericay, 75; in 'Central' District, 11, 21; factors affecting intervention in local elections, 10; and ratepayer movements, 58–60; sympathies of independent councillors with, 3; in 'Westwards' District, 19.
Lincoln 58
Lincolnshire 6, 37
Local government reorganisation: in Billericay, 70, 72; in 'Central'

District, 11, 14; in Cheshire, 12; and independent councillors, 2; and ratepayer movements, 60–61, 86, 97, 101–2; in Seaton, 80; in Walsall, 98; in 'Westwards' District, 14.
Localism 1, 88, 104–107
Lyme Regis 47

Madgwick, P. 8
Martin, E. 7
Martin, W.T. 63
Merioneth 7
Merthyr Tydfil 58
Ministerialism 29–35
Moller, D. 102
Montgomery 7
Morris and Mogey 64

Nationalist parties 3, 9, 60, 74
National Association of Ratepayer Action Groups 86
National Union of Ratepayer Associations 86, 87
Newton, K. 4, 7, 18, 22, 23, 24–25, 26, 29, 38, 102, 103, 104
Norfolk 37
Northamptonshire 37, 86
Northumberland Voters Association 40
Norway 9
Nottinghamshire 37

Olson, M. 66
Oxfordshire 7, 37

Pahl, R. 47
Parkin, F. 57
Party Politics in local government 1, 20–21, 88–95
Pembroke 7
Penn Ratepayers' Association 48
Plaid Cymru 60
Political occupations 17, 19
Powys 2, 9

Proportional representation 106–7, 108

Radnor 7
Rasmussen, J.S. 65
Ratepayers' associations: as pressure groups, 4, 46; characteristics of activists, 44, 68, 72; councillors elected by, 72, 75–76, 81, 101; councillors' perceptions of, 24–25; factors affecting electoral success, 42–45; ideologies of, 72 –74, 79–80, 89–91, 100; motivations of activists, 67–69. *See also* Billericay Residents' Association.
Rates and rating system 2, 72, 80, 86–88, 95–97, 106
Redcliffe-Maud Commission 90
Retirement communities 50–55, 77–82
Robbins, J.H. 7
Rosow, I. 52–53
Rutland 6

Salop 2, 6
Scaff, A.H. 63
Scotland 3, 9, 108
Shannas, E. 45
Sharpe, L.J. 59
Sheffield 57
Sidmouth 82
Smith, B. 50
Solihull 86
Somerset 6
Spencer, K. 20, 30, 38
Sponsoring groups 17–18
Sporadic interventionists 5, 107
Stacey, M. 4, 7, 47
Stanyer, J. 3, 7, 38, 40, 62, 76, 98, 103
Steed, M. 5, 7, 40, 58–59, 61, 69
Stoneleigh Residents' Association 49
Stratford District Council 97
Suffolk 7, 37
Sussex 37
Swansea 60, 97